**Editor**
Diana Herweck, Psy. D

**Editorial Project Manager**
Dona Herweck Rice

**Editor-in-Chief**
Sharon Coan, M.S. Ed.

**Illustrator**
Ken Tunell

**Cover Artist**
Barb Lorseyedi

**Art Coordinator**
Kevin Barnes

**Imaging**
Alfred Lau
Rosa C. See

**Product Manager**
Phil Garcia

**Publishers**
Rachelle Cracchiolo, M.S. Ed.
Mary Dupuy Smith, M.S. Ed.

# Comprehension & Critical Thinking
## LEVEL 6
**Includes Document-Based Questions**

**Author**

*Sarah Kartchner Clark*

**Reading passages provided by *TIME For Kids* magazine.**

*Teacher Created Materials, Inc.*
6421 Industry Way
Westminster, CA 92683
www.teachercreated.com
**ISBN-0-7439-3376-1**
©2002 Teacher Created Materials, Inc.
Made in U.S.A.

# Table of Contents

# Introduction

We live in a day of increased accountability and standards-based instruction. Teachers are feeling the pressure to have their students perform well on standardized tests. As educators, we know that students need more than just practice on answering questions and how to take tests. Students need thinking skills to back up what they are being taught in school. Every teacher knows that students who can comprehend what they read, and then apply information they learn to real-life situations not only score better on tests, but perform better in life.

So how can we help our students find success in taking standardized tests as well as being problem solvers for life? One way is to build students' reading comprehension and critical thinking skills. This unit has been specifically designed to build such skills. It has been written with the student in mind. This unit will provide your students with the experience of reading, comprehending, analyzing, and problem solving issues that are taking place in their world today.

The *Comprehension and Critical Thinking Skills* series is a tool that will help teachers teach comprehension and critical thinking skills to their students and enable their students to perform better in both a test and real-world setting. This series provides motivating, readable, interesting, nonfiction text, as well as exercises to help students practice comprehension and critical thinking skills while becoming better readers.

## The General Lesson Plan

Each lesson plan begins with a nonfiction article that has been written specifically for your students. These articles are written at the readability level of your students so that the vocabulary doesn't interfere with the comprehension of what is being read. These high-interest nonfiction articles are from *TIME For Kids* authors. Here is a suggestion of the general lesson plan:

**Step 1**—Students read a nonfiction article from *Time For Kids* authors.

**Step 2**—Students answer questions about the article they have just read. These questions are written using Bloom's Taxonomy as a guide. Questions begin with basic comprehension and increase in complexity and higher level thinking.

**Step 3**—Students study a primary source document (such as maps, census reports, graphs, cartoons, charts, and diagrams) that is related to the article.

**Step 4**—Students demonstrate critical thinking skills by responding to document-based questions.

**Step 5**—Students continue demonstrating critical thinking skills by participating in activities based on the documents.

# Introduction (cont.)

## What Is Bloom's Taxonomy?

The questions that follow each passage in *Comprehension and Critical Thinking* assess all levels of learning by following Bloom's Taxonomy, a six-level classification system for comprehension questions devised by Benjamin Bloom in 1956. The questions are always presented in order, progressing from knowledge to evaluation.

The skills listed for each level are essential to keep in mind when teaching comprehension to assure that your students reach the higher levels of thinking. Use this classification to form your own questions whenever your students listen to or read material.

**Level 1: Knowledge**—At this level, students are asked to recall information or find requested information in an article. They will demonstrate remembering, recognizing, and describing. Question cues associated with the knowledge level include *who, what, when, where, why, how, collect, examine, quote, name, identify, show, define, tell,* and *list.*

**Level 2: Comprehension**—At this level, students begin to interpret what is being read. This means they can find information that is stated in a different way than the question. They will demonstrate translating, putting into one's own words, organizing and selecting facts. Question cues associated with the comprehension level include *summarize, associate, estimate, extend, discuss, interpret, contrast, predict, give examples, explain,* and *describe.*

**Level 3: Application**—At this level, students use the information that has been read. They apply the knowledge to new settings and situations. Students solve problems using their knowledge and skills. Question cues associated with the application level include *apply, experiment, modify, relate, illustrate, demonstrate, solve, construct, change, discover, complete,* and *calculate.*

**Level 4: Analysis**—At this level, students begin to see patterns and the organization of parts. Students are able to recognize hidden meanings. Question cues associated with the analysis level include *analyze, organize, order, divide, compare, select, infer, classify, arrange, connect, separate,* and *cause and effect.*

**Level 5: Synthesis**—At this level, students begin to compare and discriminate between ideas presented. They pull knowledge together to create new ideas. Students are able to generalize from a set of facts, and they can relate their new knowledge to other areas. Question cues associated with the synthesis level include *predict, draw conclusions, integrate, combine, invent, prepare, rewrite, generalize, plan, create, what if...* and *design.*

**Level 6: Evaluation**—At the highest level of Bloom's Taxonomy, students can make a judgement based on a predetermined set of criteria. They can assess the value of theories and can form opinions and defend them. Students can verify the value of evidence presented. Question cues associated with the evaluation level include *test, rank, grade, decide, assess, recommend, convince, select, measure, discriminate, support, conclude, compare, summarize, judge,* and *determine.*

# Introduction *(cont.)*

## What Are Primary Source Documents?

Primary source documents are graphics or materials that we find in our everyday lives. These documents provide information that can aid in solving problems and extend comprehension. You will find samples of primary source documents following each *TIME For Kids* article. These documents are related to the topics addressed in the articles. They provide students with another way to look at information and knowledge on a given topic. Here is a list of primary source documents that may be used in the *Comprehension and Critical Thinking* series:

| | |
|---|---|
| charts | obituaries |
| graphs | poetry |
| diagrams | wills |
| geographical maps | money |
| political maps | tax records |
| town/city maps | historical documents |
| state/country maps | pictures of people |
| diaries | pictures of clothing |
| letters | pictures of landscapes |
| newspaper articles | signs |
| political cartoons | games |
| speeches | census records |
| treaties | advertisements |
| flags | encyclopedia articles |
| recipes | |

Primary source documents can be useful at all grade levels. They enable you to share information in a variety of formats. Students are bombarded with facts and information from varied sources, ranging from their textbooks to the news they watch on television. Understanding how to sift through and analyze this information will increase your students' critical thinking as well as survival skills.

## How Can I Use Primary Source Documents?

Use the questions that follow each primary source document in this series. Allow time for students to observe and analyze the documents without answering the questions. The questions will focus them in a specific direction. Encourage students to make observations of their own. After this, move on to the document-based questions that follow the documents. Be sure to allow time for class or small group discussion. This will give students the opportunity to think aloud, as well as hear other viewpoints or ideas.

Look for opportunities to incorporate other primary source documents with subjects you are studying in class. You will find your students recognizing and analyzing these sources of information in their daily lives. Using primary source documents can provide your students with opportunities to read and understand information presented in different ways. Primary source documents will help your students learn to live in the world around them.

# Introduction *(cont.)*

## What Are Document-Based Questions?

Document-based questions (DBQ) are a major focus in schools today. Once found only on advanced placement tests for high school students, document-based questions are finding themselves on standardized tests for elementary school students. The goal of document-based questions is to raise standards of teaching and learning in all schools.

Students are tested on their ability to analyze a set of documents, use their prior knowledge, and come up with answers to the document-based questions. This higher level questioning is meant to get at higher level thinking skills.

For the *Comprehension and Critical Thinking* series, students are asked to look over a document and answer a series of questions about it. Known as "scaffolding" questions, they are designed to help the student build a foundation of understanding which can be used to write an essay or answer more analytical questions.

## How Can I Introduce My Students to Document-Based Questions?

There are many things you can do to introduce your students to primary source documents and document-based questions. Here are some suggestions:

- Begin a collection of documents that can be used for document-based questions. You can find samples of documents to use practically everywhere. Collect maps, diagrams, charts, historical documents, letters, cards, announcements, signs, etc. Encourage your students to be on the lookout for them as well. Post these in your classroom, or designate a special spot for your collection. Spend a few minutes each day analyzing them and discussing them as a class or in small groups.

- After reading a newspaper or magazine article with your students, share observations. Encourage your students to analyze what the article said. What was the message of the author?

- Quiz students on what they read in their textbooks, but don't just ask them to recall questions. Ask questions that require them to use some critical thinking skills.

- After watching a movie, compare and contrast characters with your students. Analyze events in the movie. How do the characters change over a certain period of time?

- Make primary source documents of your own. Make a time line of events you have done this year in school. Take a survey of favorite subjects in school, and then graph the results. Create a map of the school and design the best possible fire escape routes. Have students be ready to explain their findings and their reasoning.

# Introduction *(cont.)*

## How Can You Build Comprehension?

Once you have an understanding of document-based questions and Bloom's Taxonomy, you are ready to implement skills that will increase the comprehension of your students. Increasing comprehension is the goal of every teacher, but there are many obstacles. Identifying and understanding these obstacles can eliminate the problems. Here is a list of common comprehension problems:

- For some students, comprehension can be inhibited because the reading level of the material is too high. Before assigning a reading assignment for students, check to be sure that the readability of the material is appropriate for your students.

- There might be vocabulary words that are hard to decipher. Sometimes one word can eliminate comprehension of an entire paragraph. Teach your students how to use context clues to determine the meaning of words.

- You may have limited English speakers in your classroom, or students with disabilities that would prevent them from comprehending what is being read. Make adjustments as needed to accommodate these needs.

- Lack of interest or motivation for what is being read can lead to low comprehension as well. Take a minute to jot down the interests of each individual student. Can you locate reading materials that your students would find interesting? This will aid comprehension as well as motivation.

There are many skills needed to form the complex activity of comprehension. This wide range of understanding and ability develops over time in competent readers. The following list includes traditional skills found in scope-and-sequence charts and standards for reading comprehension.

| | |
|---|---|
| identifies details | classifies places into categories |
| recognizes the main idea | compares and contrasts |
| recognizes hidden meaning | draws conclusions |
| determines sequence | makes generalizations |
| recalls details | recognizes paragraph organization |
| locates reference | predicts outcome |
| recalls the gist of story | recognizes hyperbole and exaggeration |
| labels parts | experiences empathy for a character |
| summarizes | experiences an emotional reaction to text |
| recognizes anaphoric relationships | judges quality/appeal of text |
| identifies time sequence | judges author's qualifications |
| describes a character | recognizes facts vs. opinions |
| retells story in own words | applies understanding to new situations |
| infers main idea | recognizes figurative language |
| infers details | identifies mood |
| infers cause and effect | identifies plot and story line |
| infers author's purpose/intent | identifies characters |

# Introduction *(cont.)*

## How Can You Build Critical Thinking Skills?

Teaching students to think critically can be challenging and exciting. Students usually think in a certain way. In some ways we have trained students to think of right or wrong answers instead of thinking there might be more than one answer to solve a problem. We need to provide students with opportunities to "think outside the box." The best resource for teaching your students to use critical thinking is YOU!

What types of questions do you ask your students? Are you always asking them basic knowledge and comprehension questions, looking only for recall of information? How much of your school day do you spend encouraging your students to solve problems for themselves and to look at alternative answers?

Thinking critically requires students to use new information, prior knowledge, and experience while experimenting and playing around with ideas. A certain amount of your school day should be dedicated to having discussions that require students to use critical thinking. Examples might include discussions about problems in your community or school, having a topic-of-the-day discussion, or having debates on issues that are of interest to the students. Don't be afraid to say, "I don't know. Let's check into that."

## Suggestions for the Teacher

When practicing skills for *Comprehension and Critical Thinking*, it is important to vocalize and discuss the process in finding the answer. After building vocabulary, tapping background knowledge, and discussing the structure that might be used in the article, have the students read each article. If the students are not able to read the article independently, have them read it with another student or in a small teacher-led group. After completing these steps, work through the comprehension questions and the document-based questions. The following are suggestions for working through these activities:

- Have students read the article silently and answer the questions.

- Have students discuss their answers in a small group or with a partner. How did students come up with their answers?

- Have students identify where they were able to locate the answers to the questions.

- Have students analyze the documents that correspond with the articles.

- Have students answer the document-based questions.

- Discuss how students were able to use their prior knowledge in this exercise.

# Introduction *(cont.)*

## Document-Based Extension Activities:  What Are They?

You will notice that some pages in this series are dedicated to providing students with extension document-based activities.  These exercises are meant to give your students more experience with analyzing problems or scenarios and using critical thinking skills to solve the problems or offer solutions.  You may choose to have the students work through all or some of these activities.  You may also opt to have students work independently or in a small group to complete these activities.  Sometimes working in a small group is good because it encourages and allows students to see other viewpoints and ideas.  Working with other people might also get your students to think "outside the box."  Some of the activities lend themselves to independent work and independent thinking.  Encourage your students to look for answers that are not typical responses.  Teach them how to think further and more critically.

## Preparing Students for Standardized Tests

Some of the recent changes taking place in standardized tests have to do with document-based questioning.  Along with these document-based questions, students are being asked to write essays on topics generated from documents.  Many of our students have little experience writing effective essays.  Use the information on the next few pages to help you teach good essay writing skills to your students.

- There are three main parts to an essay.  There is the opening paragraph, the middle paragraphs, and the closing paragraph.

- The opening paragraph is meant to hook the reader and to present the topic of the essay.  This paragraph will set the reader up for the middle paragraphs.

- The middle paragraphs make up the majority of the essay.  Each of the paragraphs in the middle is dedicated to a different point of the essay.  These paragraphs are where the evidence and the support are presented.  They should be clear and concise.

- The closing paragraph should tie all the important points together.  It should restate the point of the essay and should leave the reader with a clear idea of the essay's importance.

## Types of Essays

There are different types of essays for different purposes.  There are cause/effect essays, problem/solution essays, informative essays, points of view essays, and comparison/contrast essays.  The type of essay that you will be writing should be selected before you begin.

# Introduction *(cont.)*

## Graphic Organizers

Graphic organizers can aid students with comprehension. They can help students comprehend more and, in turn, gain insight into how to comprehend future readings. This process teaches students to connect new information to prior knowledge that is stored in his or her brain. Different types of graphic organizers can be used for different purposes. Graphic organizers can be used to organize information for writing an essay. Here are some examples of graphic organizers that can be used:

**Semantic Map**—This organizer builds vocabulary. A word for study is placed in the center of the page and four categories are made around it. The categories expand on the nature of the word and relate it back to personal knowledge and experience of the students.

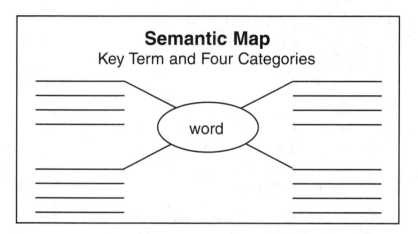

**Spider Map (Word Web)**—The topic concept, or theme is placed in the middle of the page. Like a spider's web, thoughts and ideas come out from the center, beginning with main ideas and flowing out to details.

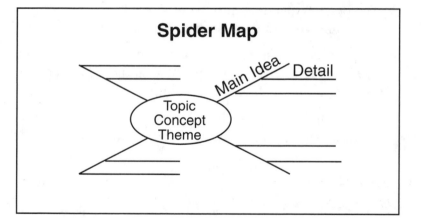

**Chain of Events**—This organizer not only shows the progression of time but also emphasizes cause and effect. Beginning with the initiating event inside of a box, subsequent arrows and boxes follow showing the events in order.

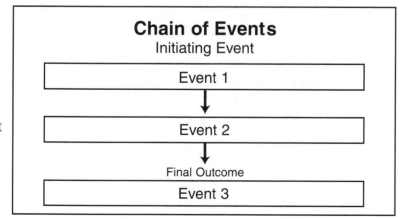

# Introduction *(cont.)*

**Venn Diagram**—This organizer compares and contrasts two ideas. With two large circles intersecting, each circle represents a different topic. The area of each circle that does not intersect is for ideas and concepts that are only true about one topic. The intersection is for ideas and concepts that are true about both topics.

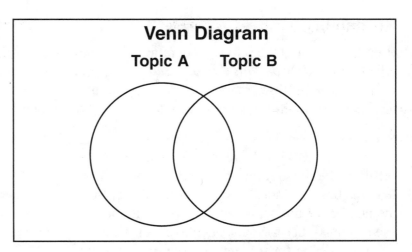

**Fishbone Diagram**—This organizer deals with cause and effect. The result is listed first, branching out in a fishbone pattern with the causes that lead up to the result, along with other effects that happened along the way.

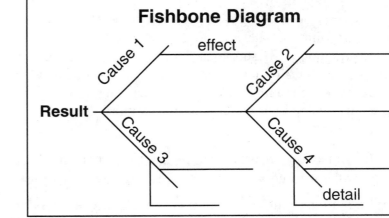

Continuum organizers can be linear or circular and contain a chain of events. These include time lines, chains of events, multiple linear maps, and circular or repeating maps.

**Time Lines**—Whether graphing ancient history or the last hour, time lines help students to see how events have progressed and to understand patterns in history.

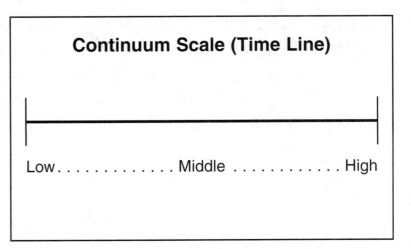

# Introduction *(cont.)*

## Readability

It is important to take into consideration the readability if you are looking to improve comprehension. All of the *TIME For Kids* articles used in this series have been edited for readability. Readability formulas look at three main variables: the number of words, syllables, and sentences. Most computers now have readability formulas available on the hard drive to determine the readability of a reading text.

Readability formulas are meant to help determine whether a selection of reading material is at the appropriate level for the reader. Readability takes into consideration the book features, the text features, the illustrations, the language and sentence features, and the story features. Each of these features become more complex as the level of readability increases. The number of words on a page, the number of unknown words, and the number of sentences can also affect readability. Through the use of readability formulas, the levels of the articles presented in this series are appropriate and comprehensible for students at each grade level.

## Using Pre-reading Strategies

Regular use of pre-reading strategies can not only help your students comprehend what they are currently reading, but these strategies can also become life-long habits that will aid in comprehension through adulthood. Be sure to stress the importance of using these strategies to your students. Many students lose points on DBQs and other tests because they don't have the ability to prepare adequately for what they are reading. They don't focus on the details or the directions. Some simple steps can help them develop their patterns of observation. Here are some pre-reading strategies to suggest to your students:

- Know exactly what the reading assignment is, and what you are looking for while you read. Look over the reading assignment. Are there any words you don't know?

- Be familiar with the resources available in your classroom or school library to help you as you read. Some of these resources might include dictionaries, encyclopedias, the Internet, and the index, glossary, etc., in your textbooks.

- Read the titles and headings. Use them to ask yourself questions about what the main idea is and what might be coming up next.

- Try to determine the main idea of each paragraph or chapter. Clearly understanding the main idea can help you focus better on questions later.

- Look closely at maps, graphics, charts, diagrams, and other illustrations to help you understand and remember important information.

- Use all of your senses when you read. What do you picture, hear, smell, etc., while you read?

- Take your time when you come across difficult passages. Reread portions that are unclear or confusing.

# Introduction (cont.)

## Vocabulary Preparation

It is important to prepare your students about vocabulary words that may be new or hard to understand prior to assigning reading. Be sure to read through each of these articles first to be aware of words that might be unknown or difficult for your students to understand. Here are some helpful tips to share with your students when they run across words they don't know:

- Look for comparisons or contrasts used in the sentence.

- Look ahead to see if a definition is included in the sentence.

- Look for other words used in the sentence that might hint at the meaning. For example, there might be synonyms or antonyms used in the sentence that indicate the meaning of a word.

- Look for words in a series. If you know the other words in the series, it might help you figure out the meaning of the word.

- Know what kind of word it is. Is it a verb? A noun? An adjective? Sometimes knowing that it is just a foreign word for the name of something doesn't distract from the meaning of the word.

## Building Student Vocabulary

Providing your students with strategies they can use to increase their vocabulary not only helps them with the immediate assignment, but also will enable them to overcome future vocabulary hurdles. Try to incorporate the use of the following vocabulary-building strategies in your classroom:

- **Dictionary/Thesaurus**—Be familiar with a dictionary and know how to use one. When all else fails, look it up in the dictionary! This may seem old-fashioned, but it can save time and energy. A thesaurus is another resource available to students, if they know how to effectively use one.

- **Context Clues**—Use context clues to determine the meaning of a word. All words rely on other words in the sentence to make sense. Good readers use context clues regularly and are aware of the different types.

- **Synonyms and Antonyms**—The study of these related words provides a structure for meaning and is also good practice for learning and building vocabulary.

- **Brainstorming**—The use of graphic organizers to list words and ideas can improve vocabulary. Anticipating the types of words and ideas that will appear in the text will help with fluency of reading as well as comprehension.

- **Word Roots and Origins**—The study of these, as well as affixes, will help students to deduce new words. Students can ask themselves, "Does it look like a word I already know? Can I figure out the meaning in the given context?"

- **Semantic Association**—Students brainstorm a list of words associated with a familiar word, sharing each other's knowledge of vocabulary and discussing less familiar words.

# Introduction *(cont.)*

## Standardized Tests

Standardized tests have become of great importance in education today. As an educator, you are able to see first-hand the benefits and the tradeoffs of this emphasis on standardized testing. You also are aware that standardized tests do not always paint an accurate picture of what your students know or of their abilities. There are many factors that are not taken into consideration when standardized tests are implemented. Some of these factors include the diversity of our country and the experiences of our students, students who do not speak English fluently and therefore cannot understand the directions, and students who live in at-risk areas and therefore do not receive the experiences necessary to perform well on the tests.

## Test Success

With the emphasis on standardized tests, there are some things you can do to help your students find success in test taking. The ability to do well when taking traditional standardized tests for comprehension requires at least three things, as follows:

- a large vocabulary of sight words

- the mastery of certain test-taking skills

- the ability to recognize and control stress

## Test-taking Skills

As a teacher you can make a difference in how your students will perform on the standardized tests. You may not change the amount of questions your students get right or wrong, but you can do many things that will better prepare them for the tests. Here are a few suggestions:

- Begin teaching test-taking strategies at the beginning of the year. Teach students to break down the directions and translate them into easy, understandable words. Use this series to show students examples of questions that might appear on the test.

- Explain the importance of having the right attitude about taking tests. Encourage students to have an "I think I can do it" thought as opposed to, "There's no use in even trying. It's too hard."

- Show students how to decipher the correct answer from the wrong or "almost" correct answers. Show students how to narrow down the answer when they are debating between answers.

- Demonstrate and practice "test etiquette": no talking, active listening, and following directions. Show students how to work within a time frame and how to budget their allotted time for tests.

- Allow time to discuss what it feels like to take tests. Have a class discussion on test anxiety and suggest ideas for overcoming the stress associated with taking tests. As a class, brainstorm a list of things students can do while they are taking a test to keep them calm and confident.

# Introduction *(cont.)*

## The Answer Key

The answer key in this book is not like answer keys you may usually use. This is because there are different types of questions being asked. Because many of the questions being asked in this series may be open-ended, or have more than one right answer, there may not be a specific answer for each question. Many of the questions require different answers from each student. Please use the following guidelines to assist you:

- If there is a specific answer requested, then the correct answer is listed.

- If there is more than one answer to a question, but the answers need to follow a specific guideline, then a suggested answer has been provided.

- And finally, some questions may simply be answered, "answers will vary." As the teacher, you will need to determine whether the student has answered the question appropriately or not. Be looking for higher level thinking skills in the answers your students provide.

Use the answers your students give as a guide to let you know which areas need to be addressed in the classroom to better prepare them for tests in the future. You may choose to allow students to analyze each other's questions and not use the answer key at all. Use the following questions as a guide:

- Which of these answers would be the most useful or beneficial?

- What are the strengths and weaknesses of each of these answers?

- What were you thinking as you came to this conclusion?

- What influenced you to come to this conclusion?

- Have you had experience with this type of problem or question before?

- How can your prior knowledge help you figure this out?

- What is your first instinct to this question? After you have had time to think, do you still feel the same way?

## Summary

Teachers need to find a way to blend test preparation with the process of learning and discovery. It is important for students to learn test-taking skills and to analyze documents. These skills will be important throughout life. It is also important for students to build vocabulary and knowledge, to create a solid foundation of comprehension skills, and to become fluent readers.

The *Comprehension and Critical Thinking* series is an outstanding program to start your students in the direction of becoming better readers and test-takers. Provide your students with an atmosphere of the joy of learning and create a climate for curiosity within your classroom. With daily practice of *Comprehension and Critical Thinking* skills, as well as test-taking strategies, teaching comprehension may seem just a little bit easier.

# It's Raining Monarchs

Have you ever seen more than 25,000 butterflies in one spot? In the fall of 1999, people in Cape May, New Jersey, were delighted by that spectacle. Fluttering clouds of monarch butterflies flew through the seaside town on their long journey south. Monarchs can fly 1,000 miles on a cold day!

Karen Oberhauser of the University of Minnesota's department of ecology thinks that fair weather helped the monarchs in 1999. Milkweed plants, which monarchs eat, grew like crazy in the upper Midwest, where there was plenty of rain.

Monarchs have a wondrous life cycle. Every spring, the monarchs that have spent the winter sleeping in the south wake up and begin to fly north. Along the way, females each lay up to 7,000 eggs on the underside of milkweed plants; then they die.

In about a month, the eggs grow into striped caterpillars, which turn into adult butterflies. This generation lives only about two months, but the females lay more eggs. The adult butterflies that grow from these eggs fly north, where they too will lay eggs. Monarchs born in late summer live as long as nine months, which gives them time to make the journey south. In the fall, monarchs migrate south to California and Mexico.

Despite 1999's huge migration, experts worry about the monarchs' future. Loggers in Mexico have cut down some of the forests where millions of monarchs spend the winter. Farmers use weed killers that can destroy milkweed plants, the monarch's favorite food as well as its egg-laying spot. In addition, the monarchs are always subject to local weather conditions. A dry spell in Texas during the summer of 1999 meant fewer plants there for the monarchs to eat.

Jeffrey Glassberg, president of the North American Butterfly Association, says protecting the butterflies is worth the effort because they are such pleasant natural neighbors: "They get along well with people, are easily approachable, don't need miles of wilderness, and they add beauty and variety to people's lives."

# It's Raining Monarchs (cont.)

**Directions:** Answer the questions. You may look at the article.

1. According to the article, how many butterflies did spectators see at one time?

2. Summarize the life cycle of a butterfly.

3. Give examples of how the butterflies' future is in danger.

4. Why was the dry spell in Texas significant to the future of the butterfly?

5. In your own words, explain why butterflies are pleasant neighbors.

6. What if there isn't enough rain in the Midwest? How will that affect the butterflies?

7. What do you predict Jeffrey Glassberg will do to assist the butterflies?

8. Assess how the author did in presenting the information on the butterflies. How do you think the author feels about butterflies?

# It's Raining Monarchs (cont.)

Butterflies migrate south to get away from the cold. Here is a map that shows the migration of the butterflies. Use this map to answer the questions below.

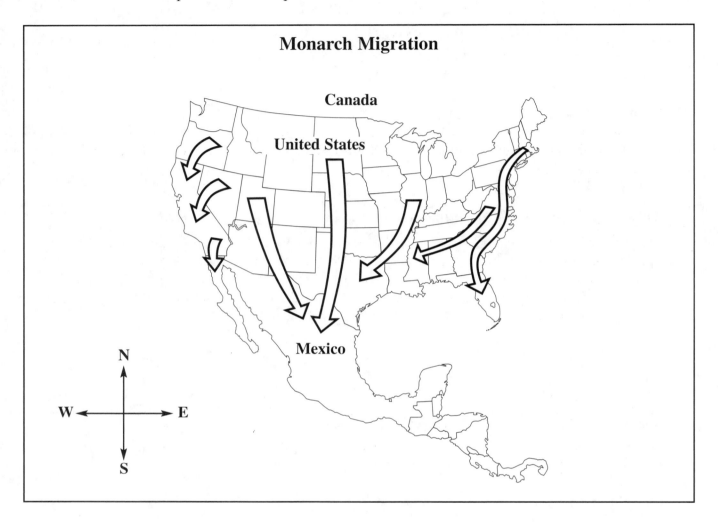

1. Using the map, tell the story of migration for the butterflies. Where do they begin? Where do they end? What things might they encounter along the way?

2. What effect does the migration of the butterflies have on the different states and Mexico?

3. Are there pros and cons to the migration of the butterflies? Why might someone be opposed? Why might someone be in favor of the migration of butterflies?

# It's Raining Monarchs *(cont.)*

## Document-Based Extension Activities

Work independently or in a small group to complete the following.

1. Draw a butterfly. How does it look? What are the parts? First draw what you think it looks like and then compare it with a picture or drawing taken from a book or the Internet.

2. Pretend you are a news reporter from Mexico or one of the states in the United States that is involved with the butterfly migration. What is the weather report like? What do spectators have to look forward to?

3. Using your prior knowledge, design a brochure that spotlights the butterfly migration. You can make a brochure by folding a horizontal piece of paper into thirds. You will need to spotlight certain information by putting it in larger, bold-faced letters and by using pictures to get your point across. This can be done using the computer. The computer will lend itself to graphics as well as clip art.

4. Write a plan to correct the dangers that are lurking for the butterflies and their migration. Read through the article again to clarify the problems and brainstorm other dangers as well. For each problem, think up a solution to correct or prevent the problem. Submit your plan to a local governing body for review. Ask them to read the plan and give you feedback. Using the feedback, alter or rewrite part of your plan.

5. Locate and gather weather maps of the areas that are involved with the butterfly. Track the weather for a few months and make a prediction as to what the weather will be like for this year. You may also check an almanac to research past weather patterns. What types of natural elements will the butterflies have to face?

6. As humans, we sometimes do a good thing when we help wildlife and there are times when we are part of the problem. Write an essay about the pros and cons of getting involved in wildlife. Be sure to support both sides of the issue. An essay needs evidence to support the idea. You may choose to write the essay about both the pros and the cons. Or, you may choose to write your essay about only the pros or only the cons. Be sure that you have accurate information to present as evidence.

# Raising Royal Treasure

It's a tale full of romance, sneaky tricks, tragedy, and most of all, girl power. Plus, it's all true. The real-life story of Cleopatra, a beautiful 17-year-old girl when she became the powerful ruler of ancient Egypt, has fascinated people for thousands of years. Now new information about Cleopatra's life is coming to the surface. Parts of her ancient royal court have been found near Alexandria, Egypt. All of these ruins are underwater.

Ancient Egyptian writings and drawings show that Cleopatra owned a royal palace on an island named Antirhodos. The island was near Alexandria, the capital city of Egypt during Cleopatra's reign in the first century B.C.

Although the city of Alexandria still exists today, floods and earthquakes buried Antirhodos under water more than 1,600 years ago. But it wasn't lost for good. In 1996, undersea explorer Franck Goddio found it beneath just 18 feet of water, off the shore of Alexandria. He found statues, columns, pavement, and pottery buried in layers of mud, seaweed, and garbage. These were the ruins of Cleopatra's palace.

Cleopatra and her brother Ptolemy XIII began to rule Egypt together in 51 B.C. In keeping with royal custom, the brother and sister were married! But Ptolemy did not want to share the throne, and he forced Cleopatra out of the palace.

The quick-witted young woman saw her chance to regain power when Rome's main leader, Julius Caesar, traveled to Egypt. In order to meet with him, Cleopatra is said to have sneaked into the palace rolled up in a carpet! Caesar soon fell in love with Cleopatra. He helped her push Ptolemy aside and take control of Egypt.

After Caesar's enemies murdered him, a new Roman leader, Mark Antony, met Cleopatra. Just like Caesar before him, Antony fell in love with her. He moved into Cleopatra's palace at Antirhodos.

Soon people back in Rome feared that Antony was more interested in Egypt than in his own empire. They turned against him and Egypt and sent a huge army by sea, which eventually defeated Egypt. In despair, Cleopatra and Antony took their own lives. Ancient Egypt's last queen died at the age of 39.

Though her reign ended 2,000 years ago, Cleopatra continues to enchant people everywhere. For that reason, Goddio hopes to set up an underwater museum at the palace site. Visitors would be able to explore and experience Cleopatra's world up close. "To be there, underwater where she reigned and died," says Goddio, "is unbelievable."

# Raising Royal Treasure *(cont.)*

**Directions:** Answer the questions. You may look at the article.

1. Who was Cleopatra?

2. Why is Cleopatra's famous city underwater?

3. Summarize in your own words what happened to Cleopatra.

4. Illustrate a picture of what you think Cleopatra looked like.

5. What pattern do you notice about Cleopatra and the choices she made?

6. What if Cleopatra and Antony hadn't taken their lives? How might things be different?

7. Recommend choices that Cleopatra could have chosen instead of the ones she did.

8. Evaluate the article. Did the author give a clear idea of who Cleopatra was and what happened to her city?

# Raising Royal Treasure *(cont.)*

Ancient Egypt is famous for many things, for example, Cleopatra and her city, Alexandria. It is also famous for its written language, which are called hieroglyphics.

Look at and read about the hieroglyphics below. Then answer the questions at the bottom of the page.

Hieroglyphics are a form of picture writing used in ancient Egypt. An alphabet of hieroglyphics is given below. In this alphabet, each picture represents a number or a letter in the English language. Note that one hieroglyph may represent more than one number or letter.

The hieroglyphics below are greatly simplified. The actual hieroglyphics of ancient Egypt are very complex and difficult to translate, and, of course, the language being written would be ancient Egyptian and not modern English.

**The Alphabet**

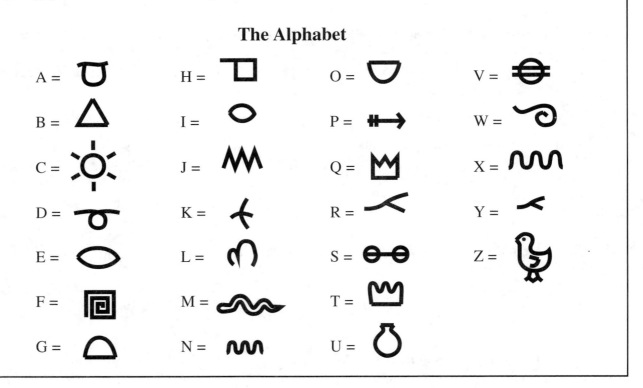

1. What are hieroglyphics?

2. How would writing be different if we used hieroglyphics today? (Think about the time it takes to write, how writing is taught in school, how e-mail might be different, etc.)

3. Analyze the hieroglyph for each letter. How do you think the letters got their symbols?

4. What do hieroglyphics tell you about the culture of ancient Egypt?

# Raising Royal Treasure *(cont.)*

## Document-Based Extension Activities

Work independently or in a small group to complete the following.

1. Write a message using the hieroglyphics on the previous page. What does your message say? Exchange messages with another student in the class and decipher each other's writing.

2. What is difficult about using hieroglyphics as opposed to writing a message with the English alphabet? How might this transfer to learning a new language?

3. Analyze why each letter got the symbol that it has. What is it about that picture that helps represent the letter? Write a new language. Create a symbol of your own for each letter of the alphabet. Have another student decipher your message using a code. Ask the student for a critique. How did you do?

4. What can you learn about the culture of Cleopatra by analyzing the hieroglyphics? Make a comparison of what you know about Cleopatra's city and the city that you live in. How are things different? How are they similar?

5. Finish the following sentence: "Cleopatra reminds me of . . . ." Think of something in your life of which you are reminded when you hear or think about Cleopatra. Is there something from her civilization to which you can relate?

6. Cleopatra was Queen of Alexandria, the capital city of Egypt in the first century B.C. Write an essay about the way your city government is run and structured in comparison to Cleopatra's. You will need to gather research and information. Attend a city council meeting. Interview the mayor. Do you agree with how things are run in your city?

7. Write a news article about the events in Alexandria during the reign of Cleopatra. Answer the questions who, what, where, when, why, and how. Write the article as if it would be printed in today's newspaper. Type the news article into the computer and select a graphic/photo to accompany your story.

# Keep the Grownups Out of It

Sixth-grader Ivory Kelly finished up an English assignment at the blackboard. Then . . . Ping! Ping! He felt staples pelting his head. The 12-year-old knew just who was dissing him. He spun around and shouted at DeAngela Byrd. DeAngela claimed she was innocent. Then she called Ivory a "guinea pig." "Hosemouth!" he yelled back.

Their teacher, Linda Mann, didn't send them to the principal. She didn't even make them stand in the hall. Instead, she sent them to work things out in a small storage room in this Nashville, Tennessee, school. The room is Glengarry Elementary's mediation center.

Mediation in school is a way to solve disputes without having teachers punish students. Kids called mediators are trained to listen to classmates accused of misbehaving or fighting. Without taking sides, the mediators help troubled kids come up with their own solutions. It usually takes no more than 15 minutes.

At Glengarry, 30 students from third through sixth grade are trained to settle fights. After calmly discussing the staple attack and name calling with sixth-grade mediators, Michael Reese and Tracie Thacker, Ivory and DeAngela signed a pledge "not to mess with each other."

Many U.S. elementary schools are starting to give kids more responsibility for discipline. In the past 10 years, one-tenth of the nation's 86,000 public schools began staffing programs to resolve conflicts, mostly in middle or high schools. But educators want to begin more mediation programs sooner. They say elementary-age kids are even better at talking about their feelings and deciding on a fair solution than older kids are! When a teacher or principal is not involved, "kids talk more freely," says Glengarry Principal Loraine Johnson.

So far, mediation seems to work well. In a 1996 survey of 115 Ohio elementary schools with mediation programs, two out of three noted a decrease in fights, and more than half said fewer kids were being sent to the principal's office. In New Mexico, reports of bad behavior in elementary schools have dropped 85% since mediation programs began.

Glengarry mediator David Townlye, 11, says the method really works and not just in school. He used his new skills to help end a long-running battle between his grandmother and mother. "My grandmother thought my mother kept spending too much on flowers she planted outside our house," said David. "I let both of them talk. Finally, my mother agreed not to spend so much." Nobody had to stand in the corner either.

# Keep the Grownups Out of It (cont.)

**Directions:** Answer the questions. You may look at the article.

1. Where were Ivory Kelly and DeAngela Byrd sent after the incident in class?

2. How long does it usually take for students to come up with a resolution?

3. Summarize in your own words what the mediation center is and its purpose.

4. How does discipline at your school compare with the mediation center discussed in the article?

5. What are the features of the mediation center that make it successful?

6. What ideas can you add to the design of the mediation program?

7. What solutions would you suggest to curb and solve fighting and other problems at your school?

8. Do you agree with the point of view that adults should stay out of disciplining and conflict resolution? Explain your answer.

# Keep the Grownups Out of It *(cont.)*

As humans, we will always have conflict at some time or another. Schools struggle with how to address conflicts and resolutions. Some schools are resorting to using conflict resolution methods that put the responsibility back on students to solve the problems. Conflict resolution requires the ability to see the cause and effect of something. Look at the cause-and-effect chart and use it to answer the questions below.

| Cause | Effect |
|---|---|
| 1. Someone threw a staple at Ivory's head. | Ivory spun around and shouted. |
| 2. Ivory and DeAngela were sent to the mediation center. | They discussed the incident with a mediator. |
| 3. | |
| 4. | |
| 5. | |

1. What does this chart show?

2. Complete the chart, listing at least three more causes and their effects, based on what you read in the article.

3. How do you think DeAngela feels? How do you think Ivory feels? How can you tell how they would feel?

4. What is a cause in this story? What is an effect?

# Keep the Grownups Out of It *(cont.)*

## Document-Based Extension Activities

Work independently or in a small group to complete the following.

1. Select one of the scenarios from the cause-and-effect chart and write a plan of resolution. Then analyze how you think both individuals involved in the plan are going to react. How will they feel about your proposed solution? Have you addressed all the issues? Have you ignored the intent of some of the individuals? Are you taking sides? Type up your plan and have it analyzed by another classmate before you turn it in.

2. How are conflicts resolved in your school? Do you agree with the way problems are addressed in your school? Draft a list of questions that can be asked of fellow students about the discipline in your school. Some questions might include the following:

   - Is discipline a serious issue in our school?
   - Do you think that fights and conflicts are handled appropriately in our school?
   - Do the students respect the teachers and other adults at our school?
   - Do you think a conflict resolution program would work in our school? Why or why not?

3. Analyze the results of the survey. What do the students at your school think about discipline? Do they feel safe? Do they feel like issues are under control? Which areas of discipline are weak? What issues are not being addressed? Brainstorm a list of possible solutions or plans to address these weak areas in discipline.

4. Keep a log of incidents that would require intervention at your school. Categorize the incidents into different categories based on the type and seriousness of the incidents. Assess whether or not you think that a mediation center would be beneficial.

5. Survey the teachers in your school. Ask them their thoughts about a mediation center. Would they prefer a mediation center or their own discipline techniques? What do teachers think are the pros and cons of a mediation center?

6. Draft a letter to the principal discussing discipline and conflict resolution at your school. Share with the principal an analysis you've done of discipline in your school, the results of the survey of students, and your recommendations. Design letterhead on the computer and type your letter on it. Be sure to check the spelling and grammar in your letter. It needs to look professional in order for the principal to take it seriously.

# Remembering Their Journey

When Frederick and Katrina Jones visit the Museum of African American History in Detroit, Michigan, they can see the great achievements of African Americans from past generations. They can also see themselves. Katrina, 13, and her brother Frederick, 11, are part of a museum exhibit. Molds of their faces and bodies were used to make statues of Africans, shown on a model slave ship.

"Vaseline covered my body before papier-mâché was applied from my stomach to my feet and later my face and upper body," Katrina recalls. "I couldn't move for over an hour, and I couldn't talk, because moving or talking would have cracked the mold."

"Seeing myself is kind of fun," says Frederick. "It was nice that kids got to do something about our heritage." When he grows up, Frederick hopes he can show his family the youthful model and say, "That's me!"

The museum, created in 1965, moved into a grand new home in April 1997. It is now the largest African American history museum anywhere. People talk about African Americans during Black History Month, but this museum celebrates the achievements of Black Americans year-round.

"The purpose of the museum is to preserve the history and culture of African Americans," says Rita Organ, curator of the museum. "I hope people will see that the contributions African Americans make extend into every facet of life and play an important part in American culture."

Visitors are greeted by a splash of bright, silky flags at the museum's entrance. Each flag stands for a nation, where centuries ago, Africans were brought here to be slaves.

In the museum's Ring of Fame, the names of 60 great Africans and African Americans grace the floor. Visitors to the inventor's area can see George Grant's invention, the golf tee. Also on display is Samella Lewis' original drawing for the design on the dime and the first traffic signal, invented by Garrett Morgan. The Congressional Medal of Honor awarded to Christian Fleetwood is among Organ's favorite items on display. Sergeant Major Fleetwood earned it for heroism in a Civil War battle.

Detroit was one of the last stops on the Underground Railroad for slaves escaping to the "promised land" of Canada. Many African Americans migrated to Detroit from the 1920s through the 1950s to work in automobile and defense factories. The defense factories made guns and other supplies needed by the armed forces to fight in World War II. Today, Detroit's 750,000 African Americans are proud that their city is home to the new museum. Organ says, "It makes sense to have it here."

# Remembering Their Journey (cont.)

**Directions:** Answer the questions. You may look at the article.

1. What is the purpose of the Museum of African American History?

2. What did Frederick and Katrina do to make statues?

3. Describe in your own words what it would feel like to walk through the museum.

4. Why is it significant that the museum was moved to Detroit?

5. How does this museum compare with other museums?

6. What evidence can you list for this museum being a success?

7. How would you design a museum for your ancestors? What would it look like? What would it hold?

8. What do you think about the museum displaying flags of the countries that brought slaves?

# Remembering Their Journey (cont.)

African Americans have made many significant contributions to the world and our culture. Below is a time line of items invented by African Americans from 1880 to 1950. Use this time line to answer questions below about African American contributions.

## Time Line of Inventions by African Americans and Other Events

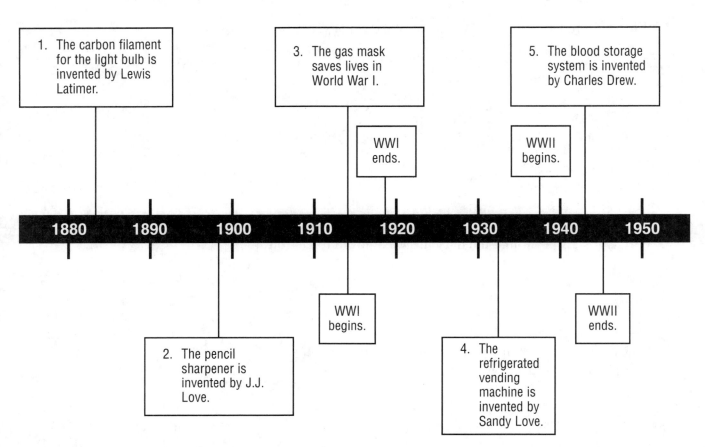

1. What did Lewis Latimer invent?

2. Select one of the inventions on the time line. What other things were taking place during that time period?

3. How would life be different without the inventions on the time line?

4. Which invention do you think is most significant? Explain your answer.

# Remembering Their Journey *(cont.)*

**Document-Based Extension Activities**

Work independently or in a small group to complete the following.

1. Looking at the time line, what inventions have African Americans invented since 1950? Create a new time line that shows these inventions with additional ones invented through the present time. What types of inventions might be on the time line in the next ten or twenty years?

2. Make a list of contributions that you know that women or other minority groups have made. Why is it easy to overlook some of these contributions?

3. Research on the Internet, or with other sources, the inventions listed on the time line. How did these inventions come about? How have these inventions made a difference? Have a group discussion on the process these inventors went through to create their invention. Discuss what can be learned from the process it takes to invent something.

4. Why do you think someone with African American ancestors would be proud of the museum? How are museums like this a positive experience for everyone? Draw up a proposal for a museum in your community similar to the Museum of African American History. What would be the subject of the museum? What would be displayed there? How would this museum benefit and educate others?

5. Write a fictional newspaper article about one of the inventions on the time line. Imagine that this invention has just been introduced. How would you inform the public? How would you educate the public on how to get one of these inventions? Why would this invention be beneficial? How was the invention received? Keep the news article informative and motivating.

6. Interview a person at a museum and find out what it takes to get approval for the museum, the gathering of artifacts, the security of the items displayed, and security necessary for museums.

7. Brainstorm a list of inventions that you think are needed. On a separate piece of paper, draw up a design of what one of your inventions would look like. If time and materials are available, make a prototype of your design.

# Dazzling Diamonds

They are older than the dinosaurs, older than nearly everything else on earth. They have been used to cut glass, cure snakebites, and charm kings and queens. Famed for their flashing beauty, diamonds are the hardest substances on earth and among the most useful. "Diamonds help us understand the history of the earth," says geologist George Harlow.

Most diamonds were formed billions of years ago in an inner layer of the earth called the mantle. About 100 miles underground, the mantle puts extreme heat (1,800 degrees Fahrenheit) and pressure on carbon, the common black substance in coal and pencils. These forces turn black carbon into clear diamond crystal. As the crystal grows, it may trap other chemicals inside, creating what Harlow calls "a space capsule from the inner earth."

How did diamonds arrive on the earth's surface? They were shot forth in boiling eruptions of melted rock hundreds of millions of years after they were formed. These eruptions were smaller but much more powerful than those of modern volcanoes. "The most recent one occurred about 50 million years ago," says Harlow, "though there's no reason one couldn't happen now."

Today, diamonds are mined on every continent except Europe and Antarctica. South Africa once shone as the diamond capital of the world. A huge rush there was sparked by a 15-year-old's lucky diamond find in a bed of gravel in the 1850s. Now Australia is the king of diamonds, producing 39% of the gems found each year. Thanks to new methods of finding gems, mines were opened just a few years ago in Canada and Colorado.

Digging for diamonds is an expensive and exhausting operation. Miners may dig through about 250 tons of rock to find just one stone. Only a fraction of the 10 tons of natural diamonds mined each year are perfect enough to be fashioned into necklaces, pins, and rings.

The 80% of diamonds found each year that is too flawed, oddly shaped, or too small for jewels is still valuable. These stones, called industrial diamonds, are used to create thousands of products, from protective eyeglasses to computer chips.

Every day, workers cut, grind, scrape, or shape runways, building materials, and streets using diamonds' hard edges. Dentists drill through tooth enamel quickly with diamond-tipped tools, and doctors perform surgery with diamond-edged scalpels.

Most businesses no longer buy costly natural diamonds. They have switched to synthetic, or man-made, diamonds. In 1955, researchers at General Electric figured out how to imitate the conditions of heat and pressure that turn carbon into diamonds. The discovery made diamonds cheaper and easier to shape for all kinds of purposes.

"Diamonds have made a large footprint in science, culture, history, literature, and technology," says Harlow. "They're just magic."

# Dazzling Diamonds (cont.)

**Directions:** Answer the questions. You may look at the article.

1. What has been around longer than dinosaurs?

2. What is an industrial diamond?

3. Describe in your own words how diamonds arrived on the earth's surface.

4. How is the price of a diamond related to how one is formed?

5. What are the different steps involved in forming a diamond?

6. Compare and contrast man-made diamonds and natural diamonds.

7. What ideas can you add for new uses of industrial or man-made diamonds?

8. What do you think about diamonds and their role in our lives?

# Dazzling Diamonds *(cont.)*

Diamonds have been around for millions of years. They are priceless gems that are significant in our lifestyle. There are other precious commodities that can be found all over the world. Look at the map that shows products and where they are found. Use the map to answer the questions below.

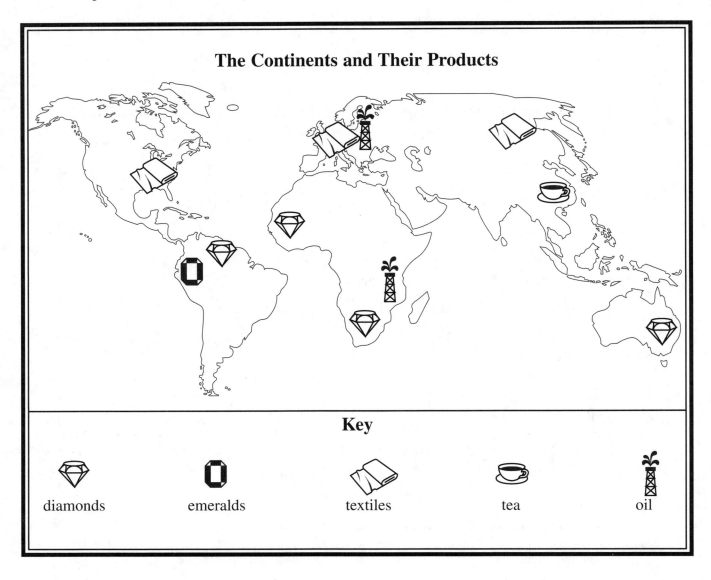

**The Continents and Their Products**

**Key**

diamonds     emeralds     textiles     tea     oil

1. What do the symbols represent on this map?

2. What do the different continents produce?

3. How do these products affect the culture and lives of the people living on that continent? Select one of the continents on the map above and write an analysis of how producing these products might affect the culture and civilization on that continent.

# Dazzling Diamonds *(cont.)*

## Document-Based Extension Activities

Work independently or in a small group to complete the following.

1. Why would harvesting diamonds be a good thing for a country to do? How would a supply of diamonds prove beneficial to a country?

2. Visit a diamond store and interview a dealer to learn the qualities of a high-quality diamond.

3. Write an informative essay about the significance of diamonds. Some questions to consider for your essay:

   - What symbolism do diamonds represent?
   - What role do diamonds play in our culture?
   - Why do you think diamonds are connected to marriage in our culture?
   - What if diamonds were no longer found? What would that do to the value of diamonds?

4. Draw a diamond. What does a diamond look like? Make a list of criteria that you could use to determine if the diamond is an industrial diamond or not.

5. Make a list of the uses of an industrial diamond. Look back in the article to locate more uses. Brainstorm with a small group for other uses. What else can be done with man-made diamonds? How does technology change the natural use of items?

6. Write an informative news article about diamonds. Be sure to include how a diamond is made and how the use of diamonds has changed through the years. How do you predict that possible changes in the technology of making diamonds might change our use of diamonds?

7. Why does the song say, "Diamonds are a girl's best friend"? Finish the following sentence: "Diamonds are a . . . ." Now, answer these questions: Do you own a diamond? Do you know someone who does? What does a diamond mean to you or to the other person?

# A Real Pain in the Neck

Carrying a backpack can be hazardous to your health. Just ask Jordan Morgan, 10, of California. "One time I fell off my bike and bruised my leg because my backpack was too heavy," says Jordan. He weighs 100 pounds. His backpack, loaded with four books, a calculator, a binder, paper, glue, and gym clothes, can weigh 20 pounds! "Sometimes I have to stop and rest because it's too heavy."

Jordan isn't the only one who needs to lighten his load. In October 1999, the American Academy of Orthopedic Surgeons (A.A.O.S.) reported that thousands of kids have back, neck, and shoulder pain caused by their heavy backpacks. The A.A.O.S. surveyed more than 100 physicians in Illinois and Delaware. More than half said they have treated kids for pain and muscle fatigue caused by backpacks. The Consumer Product Safety Commission found that in 1998, U.S. kids ages five to fourteen made 10,062 visits to doctors' offices with backpack- caused aches.

Half the doctors in the A.A.O.S. survey said a backpack can do some damage if it weighs 20 pounds or more. A study by Dr. Charlotte Alexander of Houston, Texas, showed that, on average, kids carry backpacks that weigh 10 percent of what they weigh. "That's not a problem," says Dr. Alexander, "but we found one 10 year-old with a backpack weighing 47 pounds!"

How should you carry a heavy load? Use both shoulder straps, place the heaviest items closest to your back, and bend both knees when lifting. If you have lots to carry, try a backpack with hip straps or wheels.

Jordan Morgan is packing lighter now and feeling better. Says Jordan, "I don't fall anymore or hurt myself."

# A Real Pain in the Neck (cont.)

**Directions:** Answer the questions. You may look at the article.

1. Why are some kids having neck and back pain?

2. How heavy was Jordan's backpack? How much does he weigh?

3. Describe in your own words how the doctors mentioned in the article feel about the weight of some kids' backpacks.

4. Why is the weight of the backpack significant?

5. How is the weight of the backpack an example of how things are different for kids today than they were 100 years ago?

6. What evidence can you find that the kids need to lighten their loads?

7. What solutions would you suggest for kids that have a lot of books to bring home for homework?

8. What do you think is the most important point made in the article?

# A Real Pain in the Neck *(cont.)*

The article explains that the weight of backpacks might be too heavy. This chart shows a sampling of students and the maximum weights their backpacks should be. Use this chart to answer the questions below.

| Students | Weight | Maximum Weight of a Backpack |
|----------|--------|------------------------------|
| Blake | 125 lbs. | 12.5 lbs. |
| Zach | 90 lbs. | 9 lbs. |
| Brianna | 85 lbs. | 8.5 lbs. |
| Jose | 110 lbs. | 11 lbs. |
| Keisha | 105 lbs. | 10.5 lbs. |
| Aimee | 95 lbs. | 9.5 lbs. |

1. Who on this chart can carry the heaviest backpack? What is the maximum weight his or her backpack should be?

2. If students carry backpacks that are too heavy for their body weight, what problems will they experience?

3. How do you think kids feel about the weight of their backpacks? Is it a concern? How can you tell?

4. According to the chart, what can students do to see if their backpacks are too heavy?

# A Real Pain in the Neck *(cont.)*

## Document-Based Extension Activities

Work independently or in a small group to complete the following.

1. Information needs to get out about how heavy backpacks can affect the backs and necks of students throughout the country. Using the chart on the previous page, write a script for a news report or documentary on the appropriate weight for backpacks. Working in a small group, you can assign different roles for this project. One student might be the camera person, another might write the script, and yet another can be the reporter that is filmed in the documentary or news report.

2. Write a persuasive essay that would encourage students to be careful about how heavily they load their backpacks. Remember when you write a persuasive essay, you must make the issue clear to your readers and include the facts and reasons that will give strong support to your opinion. Some questions to consider for your essay:

   - Why do students pack their backpacks so heavily?
   - How does the design of the backpack affect the weight?
   - What do the doctors and other experts suggest for the maximum weight in a backpack?

3. Why do you think students have started carrying backpacks?

4. Has the amount of homework increased? Survey three different groups. Survey teachers, parents, and students. What do teachers think is the right amount of homework? What do parents think? What do students think? How do these answers compare? Make a graph of the results you find.

5. What changes or inventions have improved the backpack? What changes could still be made? Here are some ideas to consider when answering this question: size, material, wheels, etc.

# A Million Butterflies

When Pavel Friedmann was about 11 years old, his family was forced to leave their home in Poland. The Friedmanns and other Jewish families were moved into a walled-off, isolated area called a ghetto. While he was living in the ghetto, Pavel wrote a poem called "The Butterfly." Part of the poem reads: "Such a yellow/ Is carried lightly way up high/ It went away I'm sure because it wished to kiss the world goodbye."

It was the last butterfly Pavel would ever see. He was one of six million Jewish people who were killed during World War II. The murder of Jews by members of Germany's Nazi Party from 1938 to 1945 is known as the Holocaust. It is considered to be one of the most evil acts in history.

Of the six million Jewish people who died in the Holocaust, 1.2 million were children. Eleanor Schiller, a teacher in Myrtle Beach, South Carolina, was looking for a way to help her students understand the huge number of young lives lost in the Holocaust. After she read Friedmann's poem, an idea took flight. She decided to invite students everywhere to create 1,200,000 paper butterflies to display for Holocaust Remembrance Day on April 23, 1998. Says Schiller: "I wanted kids to realize that this is a world where we can all work together."

The students at Schiller's religious school, Chabad Academy, cut out butterflies for weeks. By March, they had made about 125,000 butterflies.

Student Becky Hemmo, 13, says the project was special to her. "Butterflies are just like children—colorful and free. Butterflies don't live long, and these kids didn't live long. We should remember what happened to stop it from ever happening again."

# A Million Butterflies (cont.)

**Directions:** Answer the questions. You may look at the article.

1. Who is Pavel Friedmann?

2. When was the Holocaust Remembrance Day?

3. Describe in your own words what the Holocaust was.

4. Why is the butterfly significant in this article?

5. Illustrate a picture to go with Pavel's poem.

6. How did making the butterflies help the students in the article relate to Pavel and other children like him?

7. What if Mrs. Schiller hadn't done the project with her students?

8. What is the most important message of this article?

# A Million Butterflies *(cont.)*

World War II brought on much tragedy and pain. The Holocaust alone killed millions of Jews, while many others died during the war. The graph below shows the number of deaths of civilians, as well as military, during World War II. Use the graph to answer the questions at the bottom of the page.

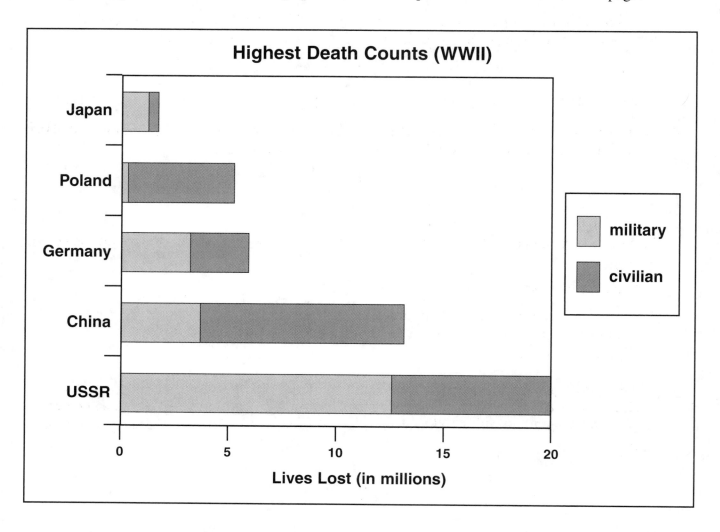

1. According to this graph, which country had the most deaths in World War II?

2. What do you notice about the ratio between military and civilian deaths during World War II? What are your thoughts about that ratio?

3. Why were there so many civilian deaths during World War II?

4. What do you think caused the military and/or civilian deaths to rise during World War II?

# A Million Butterflies (cont.)

## Document-Based Extension Activities

Work independently or in a small group to complete the following.

1. Read one of many children's books on the Holocaust. Write a comparison of this book with the experience of Pavel Friedmann. How are they alike? How are they different?

2. Write a poem about the Holocaust. Analyze the poem. How does it capture your thoughts? How does poetry allow you to express things that other forms of writing do not?

3. Write an informational essay about the Holocaust. Here are some questions to consider as you write your essay:

   • What is the main topic/message of your essay?
   • What message needs to be sent in your essay about the Holocaust?
   • Did you support your opinion? Make sure you do so with clear, provable facts.
   • How can you use the facts on the graph to support your opinion?

4. Write a list of questions you could ask someone who survived the Holocaust. Some questions you might include are: How old were you during that time? What happened to you and other members of your family? What did you learn in this experience? What advice can you give to others?

5. Set up a Holocaust Remembrance Day at your school. What things can you do to educate the other students at your school? Design a plan. Enlist volunteers to help you carry out your plan. When completed, evaluate your efforts. Did it make a difference?

6. Write a news article about your Holocaust Remembrance Day. Was it successful? Was it educational? Post this news article on your school Internet Web site. Write a journal entry on your experience. What have you learned?

# Exploring the Deep

"You have to love it before you are moved to save it," says world-famous marine biologist Sylvia Earle. She is talking about the greatest love of her life, the ocean. If anyone in the world knows what it will take to save the millions of species that live in our oceans, it's Earle.

The oceans define the earth. They cover almost 75% of the planet and hold 97% of its water. Nearly half of the world's population lives within 60 miles of the sea. Scientists say that 10 million to 30 million species of sea life may still be undiscovered.

Earle, 63, takes fish personally. She has gone on at least 50 diving expeditions and spent more than 6,000 hours under the sea. In 1970, she was captain of the first team of women to live beneath the ocean's surface. The five "aquanauts" spent two weeks in a small underwater laboratory, a small structure off the U.S. Virgin Islands.

Since 1979, when she walked freely on the ocean floor 1,250 feet beneath the water's surface, Earle has been known as "Her Deepness." She holds the world's record for the deepest dive by any human outside of a submarine.

Now Earle has a new job: explorer-in-residence for the National Geographic Society. As the leader of a five-year project, Earle will use a zippy new submarine to study the waters of the 12 national marine sanctuaries. These are underwater areas similar to national parks that are protected by the U.S. government.

Earle is terribly concerned that people are polluting and over-using the ocean. Fishing methods that use trawlers to dredge the ocean floor also destroy underwater habitats. Earle calls the trawlers "bulldozers."

Another threat comes from man-made fertilizers. They wash off fields into streams and eventually into the ocean. This encourages the harmful overgrowth of algae and the spread of toxic germs that can kill fish and cause human health problems. Billions of fish have died along the middle and southern Atlantic coast of the U.S. in recent years. Pollution is the main suspect.

Earle offers several solutions to these problems. She urges people to take action to volunteer to clean a beach. She also hopes people will learn as much as they can about how the ocean keeps all of us alive. "Far and away the greatest threat to the ocean, and thus to ourselves, is ignorance," she says, "but we can do something about that."

Earle sits on a rock and stares out at her beloved sea. She claims the key to the earth's future is not to be found among the stars. "The future is here," she says, "on this aquatic planet blessed with an ocean."

# Exploring the Deep *(cont.)*

**Directions:** Answer the questions. You may look at the article.

1. How did Sylvia Earle get the name, "Her Deepness?"

2. What is a National Marine Sanctuary?

3. Describe in your own words the solutions Earle offers to solve the oceans' problems.

4. How is the use of man-made fertilizers related to human health problems?

5. How does saving the ocean compare or contrast with saving the rain forest?

6. What solutions would you suggest for saving the oceans?

7. What if the threats to the underwater species are not addressed?

8. How would you rate Earle's effectiveness on ocean awareness?

# Exploring the Deep *(cont.)*

According to the article you just read, our oceans are in trouble.  There are problems with pollution and destruction of the habitats of many species that make their home in the oceans.  Just how deep are oceans?  Use the chart below to compare the depth of the oceans around the world and to answer the questions below.

| Ocean | Average Depth (fathoms) | Deepest Point (fathoms) |
|---|---|---|
| Arctic | 658.83 fathoms | Eurasia Basin, 2980.17 fathoms |
| Atlantic | 2,146.83 fathoms | Puerto Rico Trench, 4,705.16 fathoms |
| Indian | 2,167 fathoms | Java Trench, 4,224 fathoms |
| Pacific | 2,535.83 fathoms | Mariana Trench, 6,033.33 fathoms |

one fathom = 6 feet

1.  Which ocean has the greatest average depth?

2.  Based on the information in the chart, what do you think the word *trench* means?

3.  How would the information in this chart be helpful to Sylvia Earle?

4.  How does the depth of the ocean make it difficult to save the species that live at the bottom of the ocean?

# Exploring the Deep *(cont.)*

## Document-Based Extension Activities

Work independently or in a small group to complete the following.

1. Design a brochure on the oceans and the dangers that some species face in the ocean. Utilize the information from the chart about the depths of the different oceans throughout the world in your brochure.

2. Draw a cause-and-effect graphic to show the causes and effects of not taking care of the ocean.

3. Locate each ocean on a world map. How are these oceans interconnected? Do the countries surrounding these oceans have an impact on how healthy the oceans are?

4. Write a letter to Sylvia Earle asking questions about her work and efforts. Ask her what you, as a kid, can do to further the cause of keeping oceans clean and healthy. Design letterhead you can use to print your letter.

5. Make a list of things you can do to preserve the oceans of the world. Make a poster to portray this list. Remember to use a large font size and bold-face type to highlight certain information and draw emphasis to important points.

6. Write a cause-and-effect essay using the information you have gathered and learned about oceans. Some questions to consider as you write your essay might include:
   - What is wrong with the oceans?
   - What is the cause of these problems?
   - What are some suggestions to fix the problems that oceans and ocean species face?
   - What are the factors that need to be taken into consideration when putting a plan of prevention together?

# China's Big Dam

Farmer Wang Zuolu grows oranges and peanuts on a hilltop overlooking China's beautiful Yangtze (Yang-zee) River. His family has lived there for generations in a farmhouse of thick, mud-packed walls. But Wang, 70, and his wife Zhang Changying, 60, know that their family's happy life on the hill is coming to an end. Soon their farm will be covered by water. They must start a new life in a new village. They will have to move their family cemetery and replant their orchards.

Wang and his wife are just two of the 1.2 million Chinese who are being forced from their homes by the construction of the Three Gorges Dam. The Three Gorges Dam is named for three spectacular gorges, or canyons, in central China. When it is completed, the dam will use water power to create electricity. Its builders say it will help prevent flooding by the Yangtze. It will also be very destructive, however, changing China's natural scenery and the lives of many of its people forever.

For hundreds of years, the Yangtze's winding path and the steep cliffs and flat plains that lie on either side of its waters has inspired poets and painters. But the Yangtze can rise over its banks, causing terrible floods.

Workers are building a 600-foot-high wall that will stretch across the Yangtze. Then they will install giant generators. These will provide as much energy for the area as 15 large coal-burning power stations. However, many scientists say the dam will be an ecological disaster. It will destroy the natural surroundings and threaten many fish and animals.

By blocking the flow of the Yangtze, the dam will create a 370-mile lake, or reservoir, west of the city of Yinchang (Yee-chang). It will swallow hundreds of towns and villages. The reservoir will also threaten the habitats of hundreds of fish, plants, and animal species.

Among the creatures at risk are rare river dolphins, clouded leopards, and Siberian white cranes. The government promises to monitor the environment around the dam and has set aside money to create a protective area for the dolphins.

Scientists are doubtful about promises, however. They warn that blocking the river will create sewage backups and perhaps even cause more floods. Some fear that the dam may collapse. Many dams in China have collapsed in the past 20 years. The dam also endangers China's culture and history. Ancient pagodas, temples, and other important historic sites will be underwater.

The Chinese who must leave their homes are already feeling the impact of the Three Gorges Dam. These re-settlers, or yimin (yee-min), have no choice but to find new homes and jobs. Despite their worries, the Chinese are not permitted to speak out against the project, which is expected to cost more than $24 billion. Journalist Dai Qing landed in prison after she criticized the dam. "There is only one Yangtze River," she wrote in protest. "And we have already subjected it to many stupid deeds."

# China's Big Dam (cont.)

**Directions:** Answer the questions. You may look at the article.

1. What is the Three Gorges Dam?

2. Why does Wang Zuolu have to move?

3. Explain in your own words how the dam might affect the animals and wildlife that live there.

4. Why is the fact that many dams in China have collapsed over the last 20 years significant?

5. What evidence can you list for this dam not being a good idea?

6. How does the Yangtze compare to other rivers you know about?

7. What solutions would you suggest for the dam project?

8. What do you think about the building of the Three Gorges Dam project?

# China's Big Dam (cont.)

The government of China is planning to build Three Gorges Dam to dam up the Yangtze River. Below is the map that shows the section of the Yangtze River that will be affected by the Three Gorges Dam. Use the map to answer the questions at the bottom of the page.

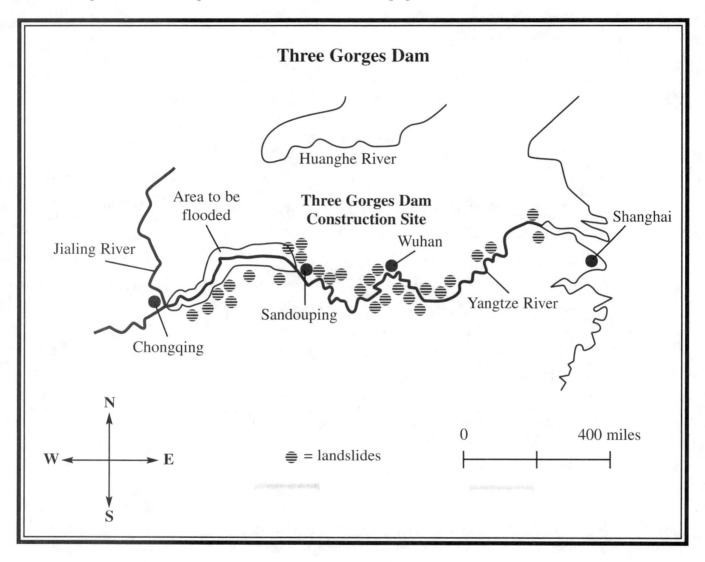

1. How many miles of the Yangtze River will be affected by the dam?


2. According to the map, what area will be affected by the dam?


3. Using the map as a reference, in what direction will the dam be built (north/south or east/west)?


4. According to the map, what river flows into the Yangtze?

# China's Big Dam (cont.)

## Document-Based Extension Activities

Work independently or in a small group to complete the following.

1. Analyze the information you have learned from the article and from the map of the Three Gorges Dam. Design a plan to address the issues of building or not building the dam. List the reasons you can find for building the dam. List the reasons for not building the dam. Which decision would you recommend? What are the tradeoffs for your decision?

2. Write a persuasive essay encouraging the reader to support the building of Three Gorges Dam or NOT building the Three Gorges Dam. Remember that you need to have plenty of evidence to support your opinion. You also need to be very clear on what your opinion is. Here are some questions to consider as you write your essay:

   - What is your viewpoint on the Three Gorges Dam?
   - What is your view on how the Chinese government is going about building the dam?
   - Are there options to building the dam that would be less damaging?
   - How are you going to convince the reader?
   - Who is your audience? How can you appeal to the audience?
   - What evidence can you use to support your opinion?

3. Research to find out the process that the United States government goes through before it builds or designs a project like the Three Gorges Dam.

4. Compare and contrast the differences between how the Chinese government and the United States Government function.

5. Have a debate with other members of your class on the building of the Three Gorges Dam. Have both sides represented in the debate. Gather sufficient evidence to put together a compelling argument. Practice your debate skills. Anticipate your opponent's points and be prepared. Practice with a partner before you begin.

# Should Kids Be Allowed to Surf the Internet?

Dear Editor,

Most public libraries now offer all visitors, kids and adults alike, free access to all sites on the Internet. Just like any powerful tool, limits must be placed on it. After all, not all sites are good for children or appropriate for them. Some are violent. Some, in the name of free speech, say irresponsible things. Others feature incorrect information for research. And many should be labeled "For Adults Only."

In 1998, there were 100,000 commercial adult sites on the Web, with as many as 200 new adult sites added each day. Couple this figure with the fact that there are roughly 200 million American children under the age of 18 with Internet access, and you have a recipe for disaster.

Back in 1967, the American Library Association (ALA) passed a resolution that stated, "A person's right to use a library should not be denied . . . because of origin, age, background, or views." Some groups argue that this resolution gives children the right to free and total access to the Internet and its unsuitable sites.

This resolution was fine in the past, but it never considered the birth of the Internet. Besides, the ALA isn't a government agency. It has no power to pass laws, and its resolutions are not legally binding.

We must pass real laws that tie U.S. government funds for library computers to the use of software that blocks out offensive material online. If the libraries don't use the software, then they don't get computers.

As a working parent, I can't be with my child every time he turns on the computer. I don't expect libraries to be babysitters. But I do expect them to work with me, not against me, in making sure my child is protected from adult-only and other irresponsible sites.

Sincerely,

Julie Richardson

Redding, California

Dear Editor,

What if, when our nation was pushing west, someone stepped forward at the Mississippi River and said, "Okay, that's far enough!" and we had stopped? We would never know the wonders that lay beyond.

Those who would restrict Internet access are threatening to destroy expansion on a similar scale. Of the nearly 9,000 public libraries in the United States, over 60 percent offer access to the Internet. But the increasing number of libraries using software to block access to certain Web sites could seriously hamper this learning tool.

Lawmakers were threatening the democratic mission of libraries by forcing them to use blocking software. This software prevents access to many areas on the Internet, including sites dealing with art, literature, women's health, politics, religion, and free speech.

Public libraries provide information to all, regardless of race, economic background, and age. What if you can't afford a home computer and your only choice is to use one of the library's? If this computer uses blocking software, then you are being denied the access that people with home computers have.

Obviously, we have to protect our kids from disturbing images and vicious predators. But that protection would come in the form of teaching, not preaching. As the American Civil Liberties Union suggests, we should start Drivers' Ed-type courses that show kids how to navigate the roads of the Internet. These classes would teach children to use critical thinking and reasoning skills to distinguish between what's valuable and what's trash. We should give our kids the tools they need to make the right decisions, not make the decisions for them. Let's not kill something before we understand it.

Sincerely yours,

Ali Hershey

Salisbury, Maryland

# Should Kids Be Allowed to Surf the Internet? *(cont.)*

**Directions:** Answer the questions. You may look at the article.

1. What types of letters are these?

2. What is the ALA?

3. Summarize the two viewpoints presented.

4. Compare the two letters. Which of these letters do you think offers more support for their viewpoint?

5. Why is the resolution passed by the ALA in 1967 significant?

6. What solutions can you suggest for the debate on the Internet in public libraries?

7. What if public libraries limited Internet use to adults?

8. What do you think about the availability of free Internet access for kids at public libraries?

# Should Kids Be Allowed to Surf the Internet? *(cont.)*

Each of the two letters that you read was trying to persuade you about the way the Internet should be used in public libraries. One claims that there should be free access, and the other claims that blocks should be placed on the Internet so that certain sites would not be available. How well do you know how to use the Internet? Look carefully at the Internet Reference Guide. Each picture is called an icon, a small image representing the type of information you will find at that link. Use the reference guide to answer the questions below:

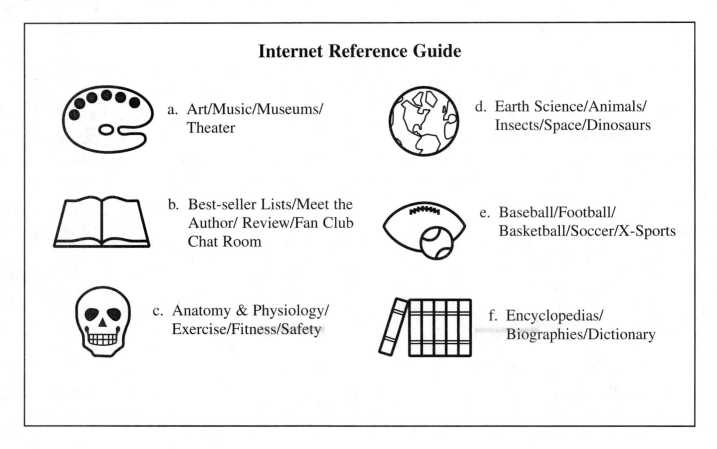

**Internet Reference Guide**

a. Art/Music/Museums/Theater

b. Best-seller Lists/Meet the Author/ Review/Fan Club Chat Room

c. Anatomy & Physiology/Exercise/Fitness/Safety

d. Earth Science/Animals/Insects/Space/Dinosaurs

e. Baseball/Football/Basketball/Soccer/X-Sports

f. Encyclopedias/Biographies/Dictionary

1. Why are Internet symbols used?

2. Which icon would you click to find out about the solar system?

3. Do pictures make it easier or more difficult for children to use the Internet? Why?

4. Are you familiar with how to use the Internet? What do you think about children using the Internet without supervision?

# Should Kids Be Allowed to Surf the Internet? *(cont.)*

## Document-Based Extension Activities

Work independently or in a small group to complete the following.

1. Brainstorm with a small group of students what information you need to determine your opinion on the issue about Internet use by children in public libraries. Make a list of things you know and things that you still need to know before you make your decision.

2. Look back at the two letters to the editor. What type of research did both authors do to support their letter of opinion? Make a list of these items and use them in your research.

3. Research the use of the Internet at public libraries. Find out how many children use the local library in your town. If possible, interview some of these children. What do they think about the issue of Internet guidelines and safety blocks?

4. Create a survey that you can use to poll the students in your school. Be sure to survey a large number of students to get an accurate view. Use the same survey to poll the teachers, parents, and other adults. What are the results? Are the results of the survey different based on the age and status of those polled?

5. Interview a public librarian to find out the history of Internet use at public libraries throughout the country. What do current laws state? Ask this person their opinion on whether or not the Internet should be monitored at public libraries.

6. Attend a local library meeting. Take notes about how changes are made and accepted. See if you can get a copy of the policies on Internet use in public libraries.

7. Analyze your findings. Write an essay on whether or not you think the Internet should have safety blocks or continue as is. Be sure to cite your research as evidence to support your ideas.

8. Why are symbols used on the Internet? Draw a symbol that would warn kids of inappropriate material.

# The Sandia Pueblo Should Share the Land

Sandia Mountain rises from the desert floor of New Mexico like a magnificent wave, cresting in a ridge of pine trees and rocks. It is part of the Cibola National Forest and a favorite getaway place for the nearly 500,000 people who live in Albuquerque (al-buh-kur-kee). They explore its natural wonders on foot, on mountain bikes, and on hang gliders.

The mountain is also close to the hearts of the 481 members of the Sandia Pueblo, a 700-year-old Native American community. They say that the mountain is sacred. In August, 1998, a judge ruled that a big chunk of Sandia's wilderness belongs to the Pueblo. But the ruling should not be allowed to stand. Nearby nature lovers should not have to give up their land.

In 1748, when Spain ruled over parts of the western U.S., a Spanish document defined the borders of the Pueblo's land. The tribe says it was given control of Sandia's western slope. The U.S. government disagreed.

For years, the Pueblo has wanted more control of sacred areas on Sandia. "We should be able to go there anytime we want," says Alex Lujan, governor of the Pueblo, which sued the government to regain the land. However, like all Americans, the Pueblo members are free to visit the mountain anytime.

In August 1998, a judge took a close look at the 250-year-old document and agreed with the Native Americans. He ordered the government to return 9,500 acres of the national forest to the Sandia Pueblo. But the readers of the document have different interpretations of its Spanish wording.

Sandia Mountain's frequent visitors are concerned that they will lose their beloved playground. They say that parcels of land that have been returned to Native Americans are now strictly off limits to others.

Samuel Wellborn, 11, is very concerned. He spends his Saturday mornings hiking the mountain with his family. "The governor of the Pueblo says they will let us on the trails, and this will stand for all time, but the thing is, he won't be there forever," says Samuel. He plans to write letters to Pueblo officials urging them to keep the trails open to everyone.

Meanwhile, a group of citizens is pushing to have the judge's ruling reversed. The Forest Service, which has controlled the land for 82 years, may challenge it, too.

The 1998 ruling is wrong and should be reversed. It is clear that many groups disagree with the ruling. They believe that it would be a shame to turn stunning Sandia Mountain into forbidden territory for hikers and hang gliders.

# The Sandia Pueblo Should
# Share the Land *(cont.)*

**Directions:** Answer the questions. You may look at the article.

1. Which Native American tribe says that the mountain is sacred?

2. Which country wrote a document that defined the borders of the Pueblo land?

3. Summarize in your own words the viewpoint of the group of citizens.

4. Why is it significant that a judge agreed with the Native Americans?

5. Identify the motive for Samuel Welborn to keep the trails of Sandia Mountain open and free.

6. What solutions would you suggest for solving this dispute?

7. What do you think about this issue?

8. What is the author's viewpoint? How can you tell what he or she thinks?

# The Sandia Pueblo Should
# Share the Land *(cont.)*

The people of the Sandia Pueblo are claiming that the Sandia Mountain is sacred and is legally theirs based on a document drawn up by the Spanish government many years ago. Look at the time line below chronicling the events on this issue. Use this time line to answer the questions below.

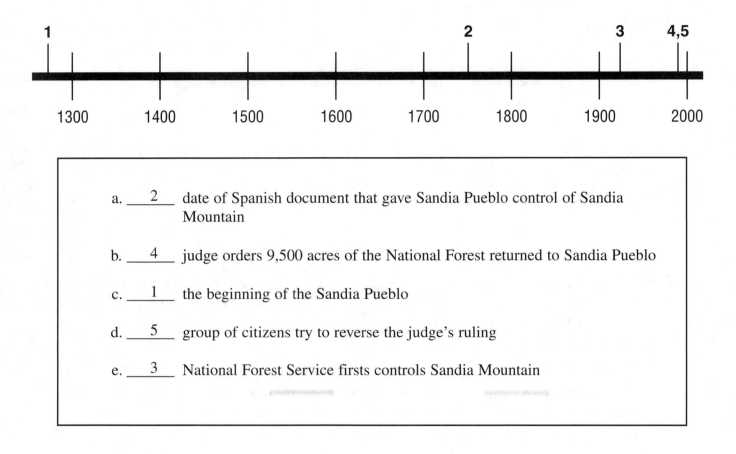

a. __2__ date of Spanish document that gave Sandia Pueblo control of Sandia Mountain

b. __4__ judge orders 9,500 acres of the National Forest returned to Sandia Pueblo

c. __1__ the beginning of the Sandia Pueblo

d. __5__ group of citizens try to reverse the judge's ruling

e. __3__ National Forest Service firsts controls Sandia Mountain

1. What does this time line show?

2. Which events on this time line would have made the people of the Sandia Pueblo happy? Which events would have made them sad?

3. What recourse might the people of the Sandia Pueblo have if the judge's decision is reversed?

4. Why would the National Forest Service be interested in keeping control of Sandia Mountain?

# The Sandia Pueblo Should Share the Land *(cont.)*

## Document-Based Extension Activities

Work independently or in a small group to complete the following.

1. Why are documents that have been signed in the past relevant today? The Declaration of Independence is a document that was signed many years ago, but is still applicable and relevant today. How is it relevant? What other documents have been signed in the past and are still used and relevant today?

2. Summarize the two main points of the Sandia Mountain debate. List the options that each group can exercise in order to get their way. As a third party, what would you suggest to both sides? Is there room for compromise?

3. Research the topic of Sandia Mountain on the Internet. Find articles and evidence supporting both sides. With a small group of students, discuss both sides of the issue. Some points/questions to consider for your discussion might be:

   - Clarify the viewpoints on both sides of the issue.
   - What evidence is there to support each side?
   - Who do you think has a stronger case?
   - What are some options that could be considered for a compromise?
   - Do you think a compromise can happen?

4. Write an essay on the viewpoint you think has the strongest case. Be sure to clearly state your viewpoint and to support it with evidence.

5. There have been other disputes between Native Americans and other groups, including the federal government, over land rights. Research some of these other cases. How can the information from these different cases help solve the issue at hand with Sandia Mountain? How are things similar or different?

# Tragedy in the Jungle

Within the lush Melghat rain forest in central India lives a colony of magnificent but endangered beasts—70 Bengal tigers. They are the last of hundreds that roamed the region less that 100 years ago. The Indian government has passed laws to protect the tigers. But there's a big problem: the laws threaten human lives.

The tigers of the Melghat Tiger Reserve share the area with the Korku, a tribe of forest dwellers. To protect the tigers, the government has barred the Korku from using the Melghat. The government wants to move 11 Korku villages out of the reserve. An additional 39 villages, which are on the fringes, will be allowed to remain. But villagers may no longer gather firewood or food or graze cattle in the reserve.

For the Korku, the laws are a threat to their very survival. Once nomadic, the Korku were forced to live in settlements in the 19th century when Britain ruled India. They became farmers, but depended on the forest for fruits, nuts, roots, and firewood.

It is a difficult way of life. Since 1993, hundreds of Korku children have died because they did not have enough food. Without the reserves' resources, even more would perish.

"The officials keep talking about saving the tiger. Don't they care about people?" asks Sonaji Dhande, a farmer. "If we leave the forest, our Korku tradition will vanish."

The Korku's plight is reflected across India. At least eight million people live in or around India's 23 tiger reserves. The reserves are home to 3,000 tigers that have managed to survive illegal hunting and the destruction of their habitat. Now, conservation laws are making it hard for humans and tigers to live together.

In January of 1997, the government decided to stop forcing villagers to move out of the reserve. It wants them to move voluntarily. Under the Indian constitution, the government must provide food, shelter, schooling, and medical care for the children of tribal people, a promise not always kept.

Conservationists admit they do not know what to do with the villagers. "There is so much hunger outside the reserves. Where do we settle them?" asks P. K. Sen, director of Project Tiger, India's program to save tigers.

The villagers of the Melghat insist that they are not a threat to the great cats that have been their neighbors for so many years. "We have no quarrel with the tiger," says Onkar Shikari, an elderly Korku. "We respect one another."

# Tragedy in the Jungle *(cont.)*

**Directions:** Answer the questions. You may look at the article.

1. In what country does the tragedy mentioned in this article take place?

2. When did the Indian government decide to stop forcing villagers out?

3. Summarize the issue in your own words.

4. Illustrate a picture of what a Korku village might look like.

5. What ideas can you add to solutions already mentioned in the article?

6. What if the villagers stay in the Reserve? What do you think will happen to the tigers?

7. Do you agree with the Indian government? Why or why not?

8. Place the following in order of priority: the Indian children, the tigers, the Indian government, the Reserve, the Korku village.

# Tragedy in the Jungle *(cont.)*

The picture below is a fictional illustration of people from the Korku village in India. At one time in the Nineteenth century, when Britain ruled India, these people were nomads forced to live in settlements. Use the picture below to answer the questions at the bottom of the page.

1. What are the people doing in the picture?

2. What can you learn from this picture about the lifestyle of the Korku villagers?

3. Do the Korku people have a primitive lifestyle? Explain your answer.

4. Looking at the picture, what would be the danger for tigers living near the village?

# Tragedy in the Jungle *(cont.)*

## Document-Based Extension Activities

Work independently or in a small group to complete the following.

1. Based on the picture and the information in the article, do you think the changes to the Korku villagers are necessary to save the tigers? When do you think the protection of animals should surpass the needs of people? When does the protection of wildlife go too far?

2. What criteria could be used to determine when people should step in to save wildlife? What are the pros and cons of intervening on behalf of wildlife – whether plants or animals?

3. What laws have been passed in your area concerning the protection of wildlife? How do these laws compare or contrast with those written by the Indian government?

4. Write an essay expressing your opinion of the Korku villagers and the Bengal tigers.

5. Design a poster that Korku villagers could post to try and save their village.

6. Write a journal entry as if you were a member from the Korku village. What would it feel like to be forced to leave your home? How would you feel about the tigers?

7. Research the Bengal tiger. Where can these animals be found? What do they eat? What do they need to survive? Why are they threatened? What is their habitat like? Has this type of tiger been bred in captivity? Analyze your findings. What suggestions can you make to the Indian government about what to do with the Bengal tigers that are being threatened?

8. Look back at the article, "Tragedy in the Jungle," and underline examples that you can use to show how the Korku villages need to be taken into consideration. What other options can be considered to allow the Korku villagers and the tigers to share the Reserve?

# Amazon Alert!

The lush Amazon rain forest stretches about 2.7 million square miles. Brightly colored parrots, swift jaguars, and fierce piranhas make their home in the tropical forest and its many rivers. Monkeys swing among high branches and vines. The Amazon holds one-fifth of the planet's freshwater supply and the world's widest variety of life.

For decades, this wildlife wonderland has been shrinking as farmers and others clear the land. In early 1998, Brazil's government confirmed what environmentalists have feared: the 1990s were a terrible decade for the rain forest. The destruction of the forest in Brazil reached record levels in 1995. In that year alone, 11,200 square miles were burned or cleared. That's nearly twice what was lost in 1994. Overall, one-eighth of the giant rain forest has been destroyed.

The bad news from Brazil was followed by a ray of hope. Brazil promised to do a better job enforcing laws that protect its natural treasure.

Loggers, miners, and farmers from Brazil and nearby countries have been rapidly moving into the Amazon since the 1960s. Some cut down trees for wood and paper. Others simply burn the forest to clear the land. Construction of roads and airplane runways has also damaged the region. The loss of trees is called "deforestation."

Space satellites regularly take pictures of the Amazon. The information released by Brazil was based on these pictures. Deforestation slowed down in 1995 and 1997. But that's not necessarily because people were protecting the forest. It's because heavy rainfall made it harder to burn trees. "These numbers are no reason to celebrate," admits Brazil's Environment Minister, Gustavo Krause.

Stephan Schwartzman of the Environmental Defense Fund calls the pace of destruction "alarming." He and other scientists are worried that they will run out of time to study the plants and animals of the rich forest. "The great tragedy is how much isn't known," he says.

To slow down deforestation, Brazil decided to get tougher on people who abuse the Amazon. In 1996, Brazil placed limits on clearing land in the region. But officials did not always enforce the laws. Now those who damage the rain forest will be punished with big fines and ordered to repair the damage. "This can make a big difference," says Schwartzman. "There is hope."

# Amazon Alert! *(cont.)*

**Directions:** Answer the questions. You may look at the article.

1. Where is the rain forest being destroyed?

2. Which year did the destruction of the rain forest reach record levels?

3. In your own words, summarize what the problem in the rain forest is.

4. Why is it significant that those who abuse the Amazon will now be punished?

5. How did the heavy rainfall in 1995 and 1997 prevent deforestation?

6. Identify the motives people have for destroying the rain forest.

7. What solutions would you suggest for saving the rain forest?

8. How would you decide who to punish and how to prevent deforestation?

# Amazon Alert! *(cont.)*

The rain forest is losing ground at a rapid pace. In 1990 and 1991, there was a combined loss of 8,000 square miles of rain forest. The graph below shows the yearly rain forest loss each year.

Is good news in store? Use the graph to help you answer the questions at the bottom of the page.

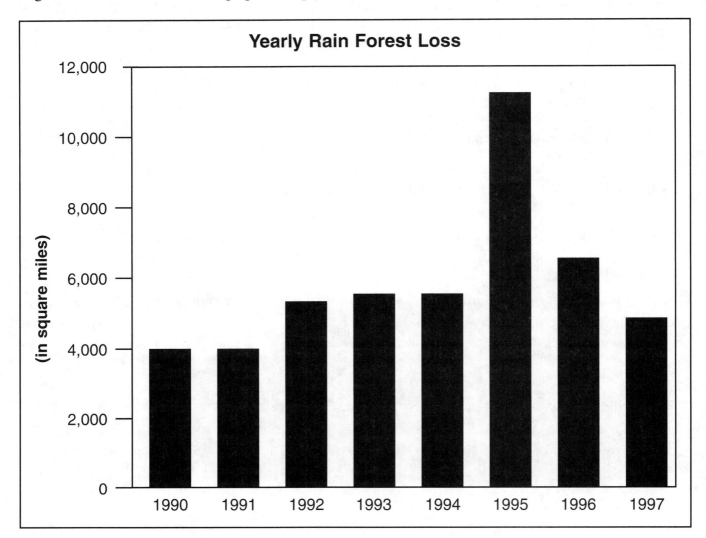

1. What is the unit of measure in this graph?

2. What year had the greatest loss of rain forest?

3. What trend do you notice about the loss of rain forest?

4. How can the Brazilian government use this graph to support their push to stop rain forest loss?

# Amazon Alert! *(cont.)*

## Document-Based Extension Activities

Work independently or in a small group to complete the following.

1. How is a graph like the one you just read able to help support your cause? How does a visual picture help send a message? How can a visual graphic sometimes send a stronger message than a paragraph of the same information? How can you use this information in the future?

2. Write a cause-and-effect essay on the loss of the rain forest. Some things to consider for your essay include the following:

   - Clearly state the causes of rain forest loss.
   - Explain the effects of these causes.
   - Use the following suggested wording: Due to . . . we now . . . ; When . . . happened, the result was . . . .
   - Explain what might alter the causes and effects.

3. How can you become involved in an issue that is going on half way around the world? How can you help from such a distance? Brainstorm with a partner a list of things that you can do to help the rain forest. Share your list with the class. See if they have more to add to it.

4. Kids have raised money for many different causes. Some kids have raised money to save the environment, or to save whales, etc. How does money help these causes? Would money help save the rain forest?

5. Research on the Internet, or using other sources, to find out why people are destroying the rain forest. What would be the benefits of destroying the rain forest? Make a list of the reasons why people destroy the rain forest.

6. What suggestions do you have as punishment for people that destroy the rain forest? Compare your answers with another student. Are your answers similar or different? Which do you think would be the most successful? Which would be the easiest to carry out?

# Global Warming

Many scientists believe that the earth is slowly getting warmer. Over the past hundred years, the temperature of the earth has increased by about one degree Fahrenheit. Is this cause for alarm? Is the earth's climate changing? If the earth is getting warmer, what do some scientists say is the cause?

Whenever something is burned—fuel in a car, coal to make electric power, or trees to clear land for farming—pollution goes into the air. Part of pollution is carbon dioxide gas. When carbon dioxide gets into the atmosphere, it prevents the heat from the sun from escaping from the earth. The heat is needed to keep the earth warm. However, as pollution increases, so does the amount of carbon dioxide. More heat is trapped, and the earth gets warmer. This is sometimes called the "greenhouse effect." The trapped warm air makes the earth much like a greenhouse. A warmer earth could cause the climate to change.

Many scientists and environmentalists believe that the only way to stop global warming is to cut down on carbon dioxide pollution. To reach such a goal, people throughout the world would have to cooperate and look for new ways to reduce pollution.

# Global Warming (cont.)

**Directions:** Answer the questions. You may look at the article.

1. What has the temperature of the earth done over the past 100 years?

2. Who believes the earth is getting warmer?

3. Summarize in your own words what global warming is.

4. How is carbon dioxide related to global warming?

5. What are the parts that make up the "greenhouse effect?"

6. What do you predict will happen with global warming in the future? Why?

7. Do you agree with scientists who believe in global warming?

8. What is the most important thing you can do to prevent global warming?

# Global Warming *(cont.)*

Some scientists believe that the world is getting warmer. The term for this is global warming. It is hard for scientists to prove this theory, but evidence is mounting. Global warming has become a topic of conversation for the average person. Look at the two cartoons below on the topic of global warming. Use the cartoons to answer the questions below.

1. Why is the boy in Cartoon A asking his dad about global warming?


2. How does the father feel about his son's question? How can you tell?


3. Do the people in Cartoon B know what global warming is? Do the people in Cartoon B believe in global warming? Explain your answer.


4. Do you have to understand what global warming is to understand these cartoons? Explain your answer.

# Global Warming *(cont.)*

## Document-Based Extension Activities

Work independently or in a small group to complete the following.

1. Begin a collection of information on global warming. Look through newspapers, magazines, or the Internet to find articles, essays, editorial cartoons, or pictures on the topic of global warming. How can you determine the validity of this information? How can you determine which ones are accurate and current?

2. Use this information to write a paper on global warming. What is it?

3. How can people use the topic of global warming as a political advantage or to push their cause? How can the issue of global warming be used to prevent others from doing certain activities?

4. Create a survey you can use to poll students on their understanding of global warming. Be sure to survey a large number of students to get an accurate view. Use the same survey to poll adults. What are the results? Is there a difference between adults and students on this topic? Why do you think this is so?

5. Interview weather forecasters or scientists, if available, on the topic of global warming. Have these experts explain the debate as to whether or not global warming is actually taking place. Look at weather data to understand how information has been gathered to document global warming.

6. Analyze your findings. Look at the results of your polling, the interviews, and the research. Is global warming taking place? Is there evidence to prove it? Write an essay on your opinion. Be sure to reference your research. Include all of your evidence and findings as examples in your essay.

7. Post your essay on the school's Internet site, if you have one. Encourage other students to respond. See what the response will be.

# A Healthy Rise in Vaccinations

Here's a shot of good news. More American babies than ever before are protected against ten childhood diseases. In 1992, only 55% of children under age two had the immunizations or shots they needed. In 1996, about 75% of kids under two were immunized.

"Childhood infectious diseases are at an all-time low," said Secretary of Health and Human Services, Donna Shalala, who announced the statistics.

Raising immunization rates has long been a goal of President Bill Clinton. He introduced a plan in 1994 to provide cheaper – sometimes free – shots, more places where kids can get immunized, and more information for parents about what shots children need.

Shalala pointed out that protection from measles, chicken pox, mumps, and other diseases is not just for babies. "Booster shots are like refilling the gas tank, making sure your immune system is able to run," she said.

With help from the federal government, researchers are trying to develop one shot that would protect against all ten diseases. That would mean fewer "ouches" at the doctor's office.

# A Healthy Rise in Vaccinations (cont.)

**Directions:** Answer the questions. You may look at the article.

1. What percentage of children was vaccinated in 1992? 1996?

2. What is at an all-time low according to Donna Shalala?

3. Summarize in your own words how vaccinations help children.

4. How is getting a booster shot like refilling a gas tank?

5. What evidence can you cite to show that the increase in vaccinations is working?

6. What ideas can you add to increasing vaccinations for healthier children?

7. What do you think about one shot that would protect against all ten diseases?

8. How would you determine the effectiveness of this booster shot?

# A Healthy Rise in Vaccinations *(cont.)*

According to the article you just read, childhood vaccinations have increased. Childhood immunizations can prevent outbreaks of serious diseases. Below is a map of the United States showing the percentage of children that have been immunized in each state. Use this map to answer the questions at the bottom of the page.

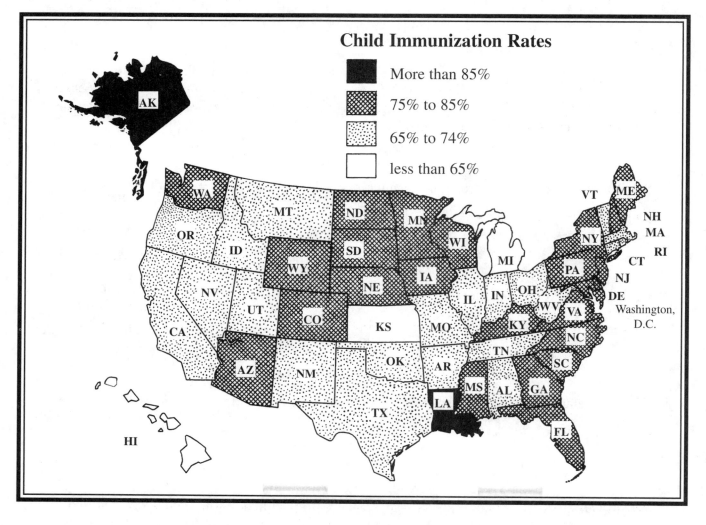

1. Which two states have the highest immunization rates?

2. Which states probably have the highest incidence of childhood diseases, which could be preventable, had the children received vaccinations? Why?

3. What can government officials do to increase vaccinations in their state?

4. What is the connection between educating parents and the higher percentage of children being immunized?

# A Healthy Rise in Vaccinations *(cont.)*

## Document-Based Extension Activities

Work independently or in a small group to complete the following.

1. Looking at the map on the previous page, what can you assume about Kansas and Michigan? What suggestions do you have for the states to increase the child immunization rates?

2. Do research on each of the childhood diseases for which one can be immunized. What causes these diseases? What happens to the body if someone catches these illnesses? When was the vaccine for each of these diseases introduced?

3. Design a brochure that can be given to parents to help educate them on the importance of immunization. Use the computer to design the brochure. If you print the brochure horizontally, you can fold the paper into thirds to create the look of a real brochure.

4. Write a letter to the editor on the importance of immunizing children. Use evidence you have gathered on the childhood diseases. Type this letter on a letterhead you have designed. Send the letter to the local newspaper and see if it is printed.

5. Write a cause-and-effect essay on the topic of childhood vaccinations. What is the cause and the effect of this situation?

6. Look back at the map. What do you think Louisiana and Alaska have done to have the high childhood immunization rates? What can other states do to increase their immunization rates? What options can you suggest?

7. Invite a public health official to come talk to your class, or set up an appointment to interview someone. What is the rate of immunizations in your state? What is being done to see that as many children as possible are immunized?

8. Using the map, write a newspaper article on the situation of childhood immunization rates in the United States. What is the status of childhood immunizations overall in the United States?

# Goal: Ending Child Labor

Carefully guiding a needle that's longer than his tiny fingers, a young boy in Pakistan stitches together the leather pieces of a soccer ball. He sits crouched in the corner of a hot, airless shed for twelve hours. For his long day's work, he will earn 60 cents.

The boy is one of more than 200 million children who work at hard, sometimes dangerous, jobs all over the world. Child labor exists in two-thirds of the world's nations. From Indonesia to Guatemala, poor children as young as six are sent off to work. Often they are mistreated and punished for not working hard enough. Children mix the gunpowder for firecrackers in China and knot the threads for carpets in India, all for pennies a day. Sometimes they are sold as slaves.

In a speech to the Child Labor Coalition, U.S. Secretary of Labor Robert Reich expressed gratitude for the organization's work to end abuse of child labor, "You turned up the heat and you got results." He also congratulated Craig Kielburger, 13, of Canada, who traveled the world for a year fighting for kids' rights. Craig believes kids can make a difference. He offers this advice, "Write letters to companies and government officials. Put pressure on leaders to make changes and to stop the misuse of children."

One solution to the child-labor problem in poor countries is education. "The future of these countries," Secretary Reich declared, "depends on a work force that is educated. We are prepared to help build schools."

Education is helping to make the world a brighter place for 12-year-old Aghan of India. When he was nine, Aghan was kidnapped from his home and sold to a carpet maker. Aghan's boss was very cruel. "I was always crying for my mother," he recalls. Aghan's dream was to learn to write so that he could send letters to his parents. Earlier this year, a group that opposes child labor rescued Aghan from the factory. Today, he is living in a shelter in New Delhi and is hard at work learning to write.

# Goal: Ending Child Labor *(cont.)*

**Directions:** Answer the questions. You may look at the article.

1. Who is Craig Kielburger? What did he do?

2. What does Secretary Reich suggest as a solution for ending child labor?

3. Summarize in your own words what the working conditions are for children involved with child labor throughout the world.

4. Why is it significant that Craig Kielburger is fighting for kids' rights?

5. What evidence can you list that shows countries in the world use child labor?

6. What solutions would you suggest to end child labor?

7. What do you think about child labor that is practiced today in the world?

8. What is the most important point brought up in this article?

# Goal: Ending Child Labor *(cont.)*

Unfortunately, child labor is alive and well in the world today. The map shows where children are hard at work throughout the world. It shows what products these children are making. Use this map to answer the questions at the bottom of the page.

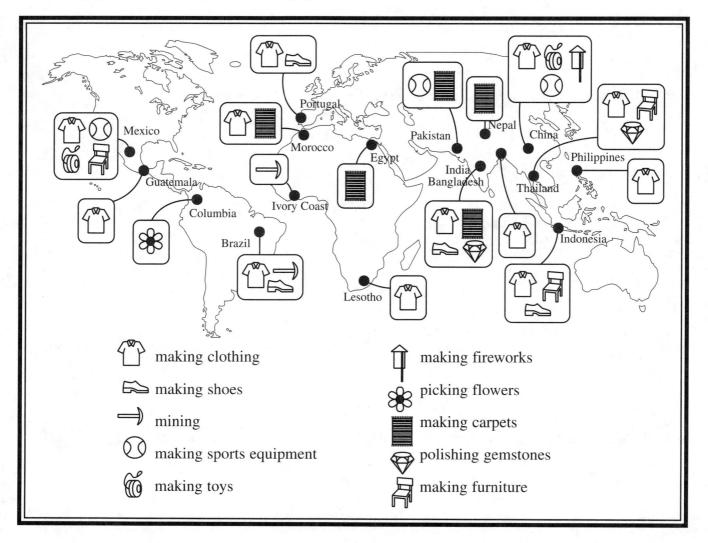

1. What types of labor are children doing in Brazil?

2. Which countries do you think have laws against child labor?

3. According to the map, in which country would a child most likely be working on a wide variety of products?

4. How do you think these children feel about child labor?

# Goal: Ending Child Labor *(cont.)*

## Document-Based Extension Activities

Work independently or in a small group to complete the following.

1. Write a statement about child labor using this map as a guide. What can you learn from this map to assist you in making your statement?

2. What can you and your class do to end child labor? First, take time to talk about how you as a class feel about child labor. Brainstorm a list of ideas. Write out a plan. Who is going to do what? How will you check to see what has been done already? Carry out the plan. Involve others. Educate others. When the plan has been completed, analyze the plan. What worked? What progress has been made? How did the plan work? Was it effective? What should be done next?

3. Write a review of the class project in newsletter format. Post this report on the school Internet Web site, if you have one. Scan pictures of your classmates and their involvement in this cause. How do you think children throughout the world would feel about your efforts?

4. Write an essay on child labor in the world. What is the problem? What are the issues that prevent it from ending? State your opinion. What evidence can you provide to support your claim?

5. E-mail friends and family informing them about the issue of child labor going on throughout the world. Scan a picture of the map on the previous page. Send a copy of your essay. See what kind of response you will get.

6. Research to learn more about Craig Kielburger. How did he get involved in this issue? What is he doing to end child labor? Where can you go to get this information? See if you can make contact with Craig through e-mail or through the postal mail. What suggestions does he have to offer?

7. Research each of the countries that are mentioned on this map. How are they involved with child labor? What benefits do these countries gain by exercising child labor? What are the conditions like for the children in their workforce? At one point in history, the United States also had child labor. How was this issue addressed? What laws were passed? What is the status of child labor today in the United States?

# A Long Walk to Protect Bison

For twenty days in February 1999, they traveled on foot and on horseback. They made their way across prairies and mountains, much the same way their ancestors journeyed more than 100 years ago. Lakota Sioux and members of other Native American tribes, including Apache, Crow, and Navajo, made the 507-mile march from the Black Hills of South Dakota to the entrance of Yellowstone National Park in Montana. Their long walk, known in the Lakota language as Tatanka Oyate Mani, or the Way of the Buffalo Walk, was a protest against the killing of bison that wander out of Yellowstone.

Bison, also called the American buffalo, are native to North America. These animals played an important role in the lives of the Plains Indians many years ago. Their meat and skins provided food, clothing, and shelter. Fifth grader Wasey Kapashesit, a Cheppewa, came all the way from Minnesota to join the march. "The walk was a way to get people to realize how important the buffalo are to us," she says.

One hundred years ago, illegal hunting brought Yellowstone's bison to the brink of extinction. Now, native groups are afraid of the "legal" killing of the animals that make up the last free-roaming bison herd in the U.S. During the winter of 1996–1997, the state of Montana killed 1,084 Yellowstone bison. At the time of the march, 17 of the park's 2,400 bison had been destroyed. The Yellowstone bison are killed when they wander out of the park because ranchers fear that the animals will spread a disease called brucellosis to cattle.

There has never been a case of wild bison spreading brucellosis to cattle, but ranchers believe the risk is real. "The presence of this disease can't be tolerated," said Jim Peterson of the Stockgrowers Association.

When the protesters arrived at Yellowstone's entrance, they held a ceremony honoring the bison. Joseph Chasing Horse, a Lakota leader, told the crowd, "Our prophecy says, if the buffalo disappear, the Lakota will disappear."

# A Long Walk to Protect Bison (cont.)

**Directions:** Answer the questions. You may look at the article.

1. Why were the Native American people walking for 507 miles?

2. What brought the bison on the verge of extinction?

3. Why were the buffalo important to the Plains Indians?

4. Explain why it is significant that this is the last free-roaming bison herd in the U.S.

5. Explain why the ranchers kill the bison.

6. What do you predict will happen to the bison herd?

7. What solutions would you suggest for the bison, the ranchers, and the Native Americans?

8. Do you agree with the Native Americans or the ranchers?

# A Long Walk to Protect Bison *(cont.)*

Bison are animals that have value to people for different reasons. Below is a chart showing what bison were sold for in 1999. Use the chart to answer the questions at the bottom of the page.

| **Fort Tanker in Nebraska** October 3, 1999 | | |
|---|---|---|
| **Group Sold** | **High** | **Low** |
| 5 Adult Bulls | $1000 | $846 |
| 1 4-yr.-old bull | $1100 | $1100 |
| 4 yr.-old bulls | $925 | $888 |
| 10 yearling bulls | $675 | $591 |
| 19 bull calves | $700 | $621 |
| 4 Adult cows | $925 | $494 |
| 5 2-yr.-old heifers | $725 | $680 |
| 10 yearling heifers | $650 | $485 |
| 15 heifer calves | $625 | $551 |

1. What does the chart show?

2. What type of bison is worth the most money?

3. Do you think the bison are more valuable to the people who buy them or to the Native Americans who walked miles and miles for the bison?

4. Why do you think people buy bison? As a pet? Food? To keep it safe from the farmers? Explain your answer.

# A Long Walk to Protect Bison *(cont.)*

## Document-Based Extension Activities

Work independently or in a small group to complete the following.

1.  Why do you think the people walked for so many miles for the bison? What would it take to be able to do something like that? Have you ever been so committed to something that you would be willing to walk for miles and miles to call attention to it? Have you done something else to show your commitment?

2.  Imagine that you are a child that belongs to the Native American tribes that were involved in this project. What do you think about the experience? Write a fictional journal entry expressing your thoughts. What do you think should be done about the bison?

3.  The chart shows the cost of purchasing bison at different ages. How does this chart show how some people feel about the bison? The bison means much more than money to the Native American tribes. How is this chart symbolic of how the settlers that came out west treated the buffalo and bison so long ago?

4.  Write an essay trying to persuade the U.S. government to step in and protect the bison. Prior to writing your essay, be sure you have a clear understanding of what your belief is. Write your opinion statement. Be sure that it is easy to read and understand. Make a list of reasons to support your opinion statement. In which order should these ideas be presented?

5.  Write a newspaper article about the events of the long walk for the bison and what is happening with the ranchers near Yellowstone. In your article, be sure you answer the following questions: who, what, where, when, why, and how. Type the news article into the computer and select a graphic or photo to accompany your article.

6.  Survey the students in your school. Do they know what a bison is? Do they understand the plight of the bison and what is happening to them? How does education help people understand what is going on? How does education help us make better choices? How can both sides be more informed?

7.  Write up a proposal that would help come to a compromise about the bison. Look at both sides of the issue before making any suggestions. Be sure that you have looked at all angles. Be sure that your proposal is written as a rough draft and then transfer it to the computer. Typing it up will make it look more professional and official. What do you think the response to your proposal will be?

# A Chance to Learn

In July of 1998, Naataosim (nat-o-sim) Mako ran away from home. Her father had told her she must drop out of school and get married. "I didn't want to marry," says Naataosim. "I wanted to stay in school." Naataosim is only ten years old! She belongs to the Masai tribe, a proud nomadic people in Kenya, Africa. The Masai place little importance on education – especially for girls.

Luckily, Naataosim knew where to go for help. She found safety at the Kajiado African Inland Church Boarding Primary School. Pricilla Nangurai (Nan-gur-aye), the principal, has helped many Masai girls get an education. Nangurai protected the girl when her father and the bridegroom chased her to school. Her father said that if the girl chose school over marriage, she could never return home.

It is atrocious that in some countries girls have to fight to go to school. Kenya is only one of many countries where girls are denied the right to learn. Every day around the world, girls are denied the right to learn. About 110 million of the world's children do not go to school. Seventy-three million of these are girls. Many girls drop out of school to get married. Others are forced to stay home to help with housework. More than half the world's 200 million child laborers are girls. Poor families make money by sending their daughters to work as maids. Some maids are only four years old!

Rekha, 10 years old, lives in New Delhi, India. She loves books and school. But her father believes she is wasting her time. "Education will be of no use to her," he says. "It will only make it difficult for us to find a husband for her." More than 80% of the girls in India start school, but many drop out. Only 30% sign up for high school. In more than 40 poor countries, fewer than a quarter of the girls attend high school. In China, almost 70% of students who drop out of school are girls. Chinese society does not encourage girls to study. "The idea of regarding men as superior has existed in China for several thousand years," says Wang Yusen who helps run the Spring Bud Project. The project helps girls stay in school. It gives them scholarships, helps their families earn more money and most importantly, changes attitudes.

Spring Bud helped both Shi Caiyun and her family. Most people in Caiyun's village earn only $60 a year. With Spring Bud's help, Caiyun learned how to read and write and how to make money by growing kiwi fruit. Thanks to Caiyun, her family makes $180 a year. Now even her father agrees that school is a good thing for girls!

Having an education affects the health, wealth, and equality of women and their children. The kids of educated women live longer, healthier lives. Mary Joy Pignozzi, who runs the girls' education program for UNICEF, calls education a basic human right. "Education is the mechanism for building a better life," she says.

The Spring Bud Project in China and Pricilla Nangurai's school in Kenya are just two of many programs around the world whose goal is to keep girls in school. With their help, parents and kids are learning many lessons. Trying to change traditional views about girls and education may be the hardest lesson of all. As the stories of these girls and many others show, however, the goal of education for all girls is critically important.

# A Chance to Learn *(cont.)*

**Directions:** Answer the questions. You may look at the article.

1. Why do some girls not get to go to school?

2. What does Pricilla Nangurai do for girls that want an education?

3. Describe how Shi Caiyun showed her family that getting an education pays off.

4. How does having an education make differences in your life?

5. Explain why boys instead of girls are encouraged to go to school?

6. Compare and contrast the three girls mentioned in the article. How are their circumstances similar and different?

7. What if parents throughout the world were taught how valuable education is for their girls?

8. Recommend what can be done to improve the educational opportunities for girls around the world.

# A Chance to Learn *(cont.)*

There are millions of girls throughout the world who do not have access to an education. Below is a journal entry of a young girl from Thailand who was lucky enough to get an education. Read the entry and use it to answer the questions below.

---

Dear Journal,

    Looking back I realize how grateful I am that I had the opportunity to go to school. I am from Africa and not many girls I know got to go to school. Today these girls don't have jobs. They are poor and starving. They say to me, "You are lucky. You got an education. You were lucky to have good parents." I say to them, "I worked hard. I got where I am today because I gave up a lot of my youth." My parents have also worked very hard and have given up food to eat so that I can go to school.

    My mom is a good example. She was very poor when she was young. She lived with my grandparents and went to school until grade six. Then she didn't have any more schooling. She worked and saved money for her daughter to one day go to school. Because of my mom's hard work, I have a college degree.

    Unfortunately, I cannot use my degree in my native country. There are no jobs for educated girls. There are only low paying jobs for educated men. I want to stay and help my country, but it is impossible to earn money to live.

    Why does my country insist on keeping girls from learning and growing? Why don't other countries help and educate girls? Don't people realize that girls grow up to have babies and without education, they don't know how to care for their babies? Why do people think that only boys need good jobs to live?

Sincerely,

Mannejerka

---

1. What is the message of this journal entry?


2. How does Mannejerka feel about girls getting an education?


3. What solutions does Mannejerka offer to educate girls?


4. Based on the information from the article and this journal entry, what do you think should be done to make sure more girls are educated?

# A Chance to Learn (cont.)

## Document-Based Extension Activities

Work independently or in a small group to complete the following.

1. Read through the journal entry again. What does Mannejerka think about education? Make a list of positive things that have happened in her life as a result of getting an education.

2. How many mornings have you gotten up and not wanted to go to school? Write a journal entry as though you are a young person who is not allowed to go to school. How would you feel? How would things be different?

3. How does going to school make a difference in your life? Make a list of positive things that happen in your life as a result of school. Don't forget to include things like friends, a community, after-school activities, teachers as role models, etc.

4. Write a newspaper article about the problem of no education for girls in some parts of the world. Research on the Internet and use the article you just read as a reference. Using statistics and facts can help support your claim.

5. Interview a person that is knowledgeable on the affairs of countries that do not allow girls to attend school. Some questions you might consider asking would be:

   • What is the country like?
   • What types of jobs do people hold?
   • How much money does it cost to live in this country?
   • How much money do people make?
   • Why are girls not allowed to attend school?
   • How would you suggest changing this?
   • What can people in the United States or other countries that encourage education do to help these children?

6. Brainstorm a list of things that can be done to educate more girls in the world. What can be done to educate parents as to the value of their children getting an education? Do you take advantage of the educational opportunities that you are provided in this country?

7. Interview a grandparent or an older neighbor. Ask them how educational opportunities have changed for children today compared to when they were young. What programs have been set up that allow more children, especially girls, to participate in education and the business world? Contemplate the educational goals you have. Where do you see yourself in ten years? Twenty? Thirty? Are you doing the things now that will help you reach these goals?

# Brand-name Schools

Imagine going to school where the uniforms are made by Nike, the cafeteria food comes from Pizza Hut, and the math lessons involve adding and subtracting M&Ms, then eating the answer.

This is a realistic scene in some schools, which have made deals with big companies. Companies are bringing brand-name products and advertisements into schools. They are distracting kids from learning and turning classes into all-day commercials. Public schools should not be making these kinds of deals.

Public schools get most of their money from state and local governments, which collect it from taxpayers. The money pays for books, buildings and teachers' salaries, but schools are often looking for extra funds.

More and more schools are turning to large companies, such as Pepsi and Pizza Hut, for support. The companies agree to pay schools for the right to advertise and sell their products in the cafeterias, classrooms, and stadiums. The companies figure that if kids start buying their stuff today, they'll continue buying it when they're grown-ups.

Big companies are willing to pay big bucks to promote their brands in school. In 1998, Pepsi paid $5.75 million to the school system of Denver, Colorado. For the next five years, all Denver public schools will carry only Pepsi-brand drinks in vending machines. The deal also gives Pepsi the right to splash its logo throughout the school. In another Colorado district, Coke paid $5.5 million to be the only soda in school.

Television, magazines, movies—they all aim ads at the kids. It's bad enough that kids are bombarded by ads outside of school. Why make kids pay attention to ads in schools as well? Such advertising encourages kids to think about spending money rather than doing schoolwork. It is not right to brainwash kids into preferring certain brands. Says Dave DiGiacomo, a school board member in Jefferson County, Colorado: "Schools shouldn't sell minds to the highest bidder."

However, other school officials, like John Bushey of Colorado Springs, argue that school advertising, "doesn't interfere with education." His district signed an $8 million deal with Coke in 1997. The money will help pay for musical instruments, athletic equipment, and other expenses. School districts in California, Florida, and Maryland are also considering joining up with big companies.

Schools need to find other ways to earn extra money. They shouldn't use kids as pawns in their advertising campaigns.

# Brand-name Schools (cont.)

**Directions:** Answer the questions. You may look at the article.

1. Why do schools make deals with big companies?

2. Why does the author disagree with companies selling their products and advertising in school?

3. Big companies like Pepsi and Coke pay school districts large sums to do what?

4. "It is not right to brainwash kids into preferring certain brands." What is the hidden meaning of that sentence?

5. Explain why some people think putting ads in school is brainwashing kids.

6. What would be different if big companies were banned from advertising in schools but could sell their products?

7. What ideas do you suggest for schools to make money?

8. Evaluate how the author presented his view on big companies selling their products in school. Do you agree or disagree?

# Brand-name Schools (cont.)

Schools are struggling with the issue of how much time and attention they are giving to companies that are looking for free and paid advertising. Read the fictional newspaper article below to see what some schools in the country are doing. Use the newspaper article to answer the questions below.

---

**Brand Names in Schools**

*June, 1998* Cannon City is the largest school district yet to take on brand-name companies. They have an approved policy on commercialism in their schools. Their policy states that all long-term corporate sponsorships need to be approved by the governing Board of Education. It also prevents teachers from using brand-name products in their schools. The policy also prevents any district-wide exclusive contract with a soda or snack food company.

"This is the first school we know to have adopted such a stringent policy," says Andrea Cronen, Executive Director of the Center for Commercial-Free Public Education. However, according to the Center, the school district could do much more and could use stronger wording. One weakness is that while the policy prevents schools in the district from establishing food contracts, it doesn't prohibit high schools in the district from setting up food contracts at athletic functions. Furthermore, the policy doesn't set up penalties for teachers that use brand-name products in the classroom. The door is wide open for companies looking to sneak in.

---

1. What is the message of this news article?

2. Do you think not allowing companies to advertise in schools is a move in the right direction? Why or why not?

3. Why do you think that soda and snack companies are mentioned exclusively in this article?

4. How would this article be different if it were supportive of brand name companies in schools?

# Brand-name Schools (cont.)

## Document-Based Extension Activities

Work independently or in a small group to complete the following.

1. Imagine that your group has been given the assignment to determine whether or not companies should be able to advertise in your school. Go through the following steps to determine the pros and cons of brand-name products/companies in your school. First, brainstorm as a group what information you would need to determine the role companies should play in your school.

2. Look back at the article, "Brand-name Schools." What did the schools consider before allowing companies into the school? Make a list of these items and use them in your own research.

3. Research how the money schools earn from these companies is being used in the schools. Do any schools in your town have contracts with large companies? Are there any in your state or surrounding states? Interview personnel via e-mail or in person to gather their input on the topic of brand-name companies and schools.

4. Create a survey that you can use to poll the students on this topic in your school. Be sure to survey a large number of students to get an accurate view. Use the same survey to poll the teachers and administrators at your school, as well as a large sample of parents. What are the results?

5. Interview the person in charge of making these decisions at your school. Ask about the benefits and negative aspects in your school. Ask this person his or her opinion on whether or not he or she thinks the school should keep or get contracts with companies to sell products or push products to students.

6. Interview the school administrators to find out what the history of these companies has been in your school district. Has anyone attempted to try and set up a relationship with these companies before? What happened and what is the feeling about the partnership of the school and these companies?

7. See if you can set up an interview with a member of the school board. Talk with the school board member about the process to bring the topic of companies making deals with schools to the attention of the school and the school board members. Attend a school board meeting and take notes about how changes are made and accepted in the district.

8. Analyze your findings. Look at the results of your surveys, interviews, observations, and research. Is your school a candidate for making deals with companies? As a group, write a recommendation to your teacher. Include all of your research and findings with your recommendation.

# War on Land Mines

Barefoot and wearing blue jeans, the world's new number one peacemaker, Jody Williams, greeted reporters at the end of a dirt road near Putney, Vermont. She had just received a remarkable birthday present. On October 10, 1997, one day after her 47th birthday, Williams won one of the world's top honors: the Nobel Peace Prize. She received the $1 million award for her efforts to rid the world of deadly land mines.

Williams shared the prize with her organization, the International Campaign to Ban Land Mines. In just six years, Williams helped persuade more than 100 countries to ban the deadly underground weapons, which explode when people step on them. Experts think that more than 100 million land mines lie buried in 60 countries. More than 26,000 people are killed or hurt by mines each year. Most victims are civilians, not soldiers.

About 85% of the world's land mine accidents have occurred in Afghanistan, Angola, and Cambodia. In Angola some 8,000 children have lost arms or legs because of mines.

William's campaign started in 1991, when the Vietnam Veterans of America Foundation hired her. The group wanted to help victims of land mines. "When we began," she said, "we were just three people sitting in a room." The group soon discovered that helping victims was not enough and decided they wanted to rid the world of weapons that have caused so much pain.

Thanks to hard work by Williams and thousands of others, that goal is getting closer. A treaty banning the manufacture and use of land mines was signed in Ottawa, Canada. More than 100 nations signed the treaty. Some big nations – including China, Iran, Iraq, India, Pakistan, and the United States – refuse to sign, though. Officials in the U.S. say the country cannot accept a complete ban because land mines are needed along the uneasy border between North and South Korea. 37,000 U.S. soldiers are stationed along the border. Removing the mines would put the soldiers at risk.

A big part of Williams' future efforts will be the removal of land mines. A mine costs about $3 to make but about $1,000 to remove. It may take an expert an entire day to clear an area half the size of a football field. Ending the danger of land mines will be a slow process. Jody Williams has vowed to continue her fight.

# War on Land Mines *(cont.)*

**Directions:** Answer the questions. You may look at the article.

1. How many people are hurt or killed each year by land mines? How many children in Angola have lost arms or legs because of land mines?

2. What is the International Campaign to Ban Land Mines? What is its purpose?

3. Explain what Jody Williams does to further the cause of banning land mines. What has she won?

4. List the reasons why countries would use land mines.

5. A land mine costs $3 to make but about $1,000 to remove. Explain the difference in price.

6. One hundred countries signed the land mine treaty, but some big countries didn't. Why do you think these countries didn't sign the treaty?

7. What are the motives for the United States not to participate in the land mine treaty? What do you think the United States should do?

8. What solutions would you suggest to rid the world of land mines? Explain your reasons below.

9. Do you agree with Jody Williams and her work with ridding the world of land mines? Explain your answer.

# War on Land Mines *(cont.)*

Even though there has been a lot of work to rid the world of land mines, there are still many land mines. Land mines are dangerous and can cause life-altering damage. Look over the chart below listing where and how many land mines can be found in the world. Use this chart to answer the questions below.

| According to the United Nations, the 10 countries with the most land mines still in place are as follows: | |
| --- | --- |
| Afghanistan | 9-10 million |
| Angola | 9 million |
| Iraq | 5-10 million |
| Kuwait | 5 million |
| Cambodia | 4-7 million |
| Western Sahara | 1-2 million |
| Mozambique | 1-2 million |
| Somalia | 1 million |
| Bosnia-Herzegovina | 1 million |
| Croatia | 1 million |

1. Which country has the most land mines still in place?

2. What do the countries on this chart have in common? Why do they have so many land mines?

3. Looking at the chart, do you think ten years from now there will be more or less land mines in the world? Explain your answer.

4. Write a fictional letter to the countries that have land mines recommending what they can do to get rid of the land mines.

# War on Land Mines *(cont.)*

## Document-Based Extension Activities

Work independently or in a small group to complete the following.

1. Using your prior knowledge, as well as the knowledge you gained from reading the article and the graph on land mines, design an informational pamphlet or brochure on the topic. Type the pamphlet into the computer. Be sure to format the pamphlet on the horizontal option for the paper. Then you can fold the paper into thirds to make it look like a pamphlet. You will need to spotlight certain information by putting it in larger, bold-faced letters and by using pictures and call-outs to get your point across. The computer will lend itself to graphics and clip art.

2. Write a plan to correct the dangers of the land mines in the world. Read through the article again to clarify the problems and brainstorm other dangers that might be involved as well. Think up a solution to correct or prevent each problem. Submit your plan to your teacher. Ask him or her to read the plan and give you feedback. Using the feedback, alter or rewrite your plan accordingly.

3. Locate and gather maps of the countries that are listed on the chart. Research and gather information about these countries. Why were the land mines put in place? How do the countries feel about the land mines being there? What plans do these countries have for these land mines? Locate evidence of action taken to either remove or install land mines. Which of the countries on the graph do you think are most likely to be willing to get rid of land mines? Do they have the resources available to do it? Write a letter of encouragement to the governments of these countries encouraging them to do so.

4. What would it be like to have stepped on a land mine? Research the injuries that children and others have faced as a result of stepping on a land mine. What are the medical facilities like in these countries with land mines? Are they adequately able to care for the victims of these land mines? Write a journal entry from a land mine survivor. What would the experience be like, both emotionally and physically?

5. As humans, we do things without realizing the impact of our actions. People who have placed these land mines may not realize the harm they have done. Are there things that you do now that you won't be able to see the effects for years to come? Make a list of these things. Write an essay about the choices that we make and how they affect others. In your essay, make a suggestion of steps to follow prior to making serious decisions that can affect others.

# Math + Ads = Trouble

Will is saving his allowance to buy a pair of Nike shoes that cost $68.25. If Will earns $3.25 per week, how many weeks does Will need to save?

Poor Will. He will have to save his allowance for 21 weeks just to buy a pair of sneakers! But this problem presents a much more serious issue: the use of brand names in textbooks. This practice is a sneaky way for companies to promote products to kids. California has already passed a law saying that new textbooks used in its schools should be free of brand names. The other 49 states should do the same.

When a California lawyer read the word problem above, he wondered why his child was reading about Nike sneakers in a math book.

"We found half a dozen or more pictures and things that looked like they were ads," Stein told the Santa Rosa Press Democrat newspaper. Stein decided to complain to a member of the state legislature.

The Nike word problem and examples involving M&Ms, Oreos, and fast-food restaurants appear in "Mathematics: Applications and Connections," a sixth grade math book published by Glencoe/McGraw-Hill. It is one of several textbooks that mention brand names.

Publishers of such books insist that they are only trying to make math problems a little more interesting and show how math relates to real life. "It's not advertising," says Bill Jordan, a spokeswoman for McGraw-Hill. The publisher was not paid to mention any brands.

But California lawmakers agreed with Stein. The state legislature passed a law saying all new textbooks for California schools must be free of product names.

Now McGraw-Hill is publishing a new version of its math book without the brand names, especially for California's schools. The other states should join California. Ads don't belong in schools. There are many creative teachers out there. Surely they can find other ways to make learning real and exciting.

# Math + Ads = Trouble *(cont.)*

**Directions:** Answer the questions. You may look at the article.

1. What is found in the math textbooks?

2. Who found the references to companies in his kid's math problems? How did he feel about it?

3. Summarize how the author feels about the "advertisements" in the math textbooks. Do you agree or disagree with the author?

4. Describe how the author thinks this problem of references in the math textbooks could be detrimental to students.

5. The writer begins the article with a quote from a math textbook. List two reasons why this was an effective introduction.

6. What do you think about brand names in a textbook? Can they make learning more interesting or not?

7. How do you predict textbook companies, like McGraw-Hill, will respond? Will they make changes in the textbooks?

8. Imagine that you read about a brand name pair of sneakers in a textbook. Would it make you want to go out and buy the sneakers? Why or why not?

# Math + Ads = Trouble *(cont.)*

School Districts are looking at the role that brand names are playing in their curriculum. Schools are wondering if the role of big companies is a positive one. Look at this sample school board policy written to address this issue. Use the policy to answer the questions below.

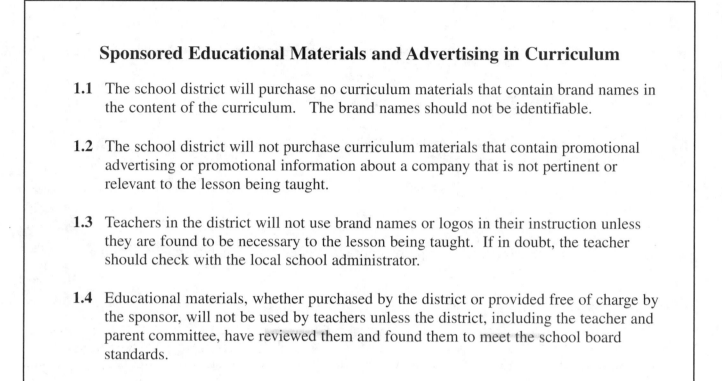

**Sponsored Educational Materials and Advertising in Curriculum**

**1.1** The school district will purchase no curriculum materials that contain brand names in the content of the curriculum. The brand names should not be identifiable.

**1.2** The school district will not purchase curriculum materials that contain promotional advertising or promotional information about a company that is not pertinent or relevant to the lesson being taught.

**1.3** Teachers in the district will not use brand names or logos in their instruction unless they are found to be necessary to the lesson being taught. If in doubt, the teacher should check with the local school administrator.

**1.4** Educational materials, whether purchased by the district or provided free of charge by the sponsor, will not be used by teachers unless the district, including the teacher and parent committee, have reviewed them and found them to meet the school board standards.

1. What is the purpose of this school board policy? Why do you think this policy was established?

2. Does your school board have a school board policy similar to this one? Do you agree or disagree with the policy?

3. Why are schools feeling the need to crack down on how involved brand name companies get in their schools? What are the pros and cons of having these companies involved in education?

4. What can companies do to promote the good that they are able to accomplish by being involved in the education of children?

# Math + Ads = Trouble *(cont.)*

## Document-Based Extension Activities

Work independently or in a small group to complete the following.

1. Do the textbooks that you use in school use brand-name companies or products in them? What do you think about this? Do you think it is acceptable to use these companies or products to motivate the students?

2. Pretend you are a news reporter investigating this issue. Attend a school board meeting. Look into school board policies to find out the stance of the school district on using text or wording in their curriculum to support or advertise for these companies.

3. Interview the principal at your school. What does he or she think about the issue of brand-name companies or products used to teach lessons to students? Is this a problem at your school? If so, what has been done to address the problem? How do teachers feel about this issue? Do teachers support advertising-free curriculum, or do they like the option of using these brand-name products or companies to motivate students?

4. Write a plan of what you as students can do. Read through articles on the Internet about other schools that are dealing with this issue. What types of things or strategies have they found successful? What do parents in your district think? Do they care? How can you involve parents on this issue?

5. Perhaps you disagree with the author of the article. Do you think that schools should have the right to incorporate these companies and their products into the curriculum and lessons? How can you encourage more of this practice in your school and district?

6. Poll the students to find out what they think on the issue. What types of products or companies would the students be interested in? Design a poster listing your beliefs on the topic. Quote students on the poster.

7. Analyze your findings. Look at the results of your surveys, interviews, and observations. Write an essay listing the pros and cons of having companies as a part of the lessons in schools. Be sure to provide ample evidence for both sides of the issue. At the end of the essay, you may write your recommendation to the audience.

# Do Athletes Make Too Much Money?

## Yes

Which job do you think is more important – leading the United States or hitting a baseball? Most people would choose the first job, that of President of the United States. However, many baseball players and other professional athletes make several times the amount of money that the President earns each year. It's time to limit the salaries of pro athletes.

Some athletes get paid many millions of dollars a year. In return, they attend several training camps for several weeks per year. Then they play a team sport for a few months. For baseball and basketball players, this means playing several games a week. Football players play one game a week. So these athletes are getting paid for a few hours of work a week. At the same time, doctors and teachers work at least 40 hours a week for a tiny percentage of an athlete's salary.

Huge salaries for pro athletes have hurt sports fans. In order to pay these salaries, teams have raised ticket prices. So, many sports fans cannot afford to see their favorite teams in person. Also, some teams have only hurt themselves by paying the multimillion dollar salaries to athletes. After paying one athlete an enormous amount of money, a team may not have enough money to pay other good players. Once again, fans suffer.

Paying huge salaries to athletes sends the wrong message to kids and everyone else. It says that being a baseball or football player is a greater feat than being a teacher, a nurse, or a judge. Sports leagues should help the public see what's really important. They should limit the money made by athletes.

## No

Pro athletes have rare talents. They can run faster, jump higher, and throw harder than other people. They devote lots of time to staying in shape. For these reasons, there should be no limit on the amount of money an athlete makes.

Pro athletes have only a few years to earn money from their talents. Many baseball, basketball, and football players can play their sport only throughout their twenties. They should have the chance to make money to save for their later years.

Sports teams are businesses. If they have great players, they will attract lots of fans who buy tickets and team merchandise. Teams should be able to spend as much as they want to attract the best athletes. And the athletes should be able to share the teams' wealth.

Being a pro athlete is a job, just as being a doctor or a lawyer is a job. There are no salary limits in those jobs. Why should athletes be limited in how much money they can earn?

# Do Athletes Make Too Much Money? (cont.)

**Directions:** Answer the questions. You may look at the article.

1. What is the topic of this card?

2. About how many hours a week does the article state that athletes work? How many hours does the article mention that doctors and teachers work?

3. Do you think it is fair to compare the salary of athletes to that of teachers, doctors, and other professionals?

4. Describe how you think people would be able to limit the salaries of professional athletes.

5. Obviously, professional teams feel the need to pay professional athletes the salaries they currently receive. Make a list of reasons why they need to pay the athletes the high salaries.

6. What if professional sports activities were free? How would that affect the salaries of professional athletes?

7. Which viewpoint do you agree with? Explain your answer.

8. Which viewpoint do you think was most persuasive and effective? Explain your answer.

# Do Athletes Make Too Much Money? (cont.)

Many people complain that athlete's are making too much money. The more money required to pay athletes, the more money is asked from the sports fan. Just how much is enough? Look at this fictional chart put together listing the ten most valuable athletes. Use the chart to answer the questions at the bottom of the page.

| The World's Top Ten Most Valuable Athletes | | | | |
|---|---|---|---|---|
| **Rank** | **Name** | **Salary** | **Panel Votes** | **Sport** |
| 1 | Tiger Woods | $63.1m | 4 | golf |
| 2 | Michael Schumacher | $59m | 4 | motor sport |
| 3 | Shaquille O'Neal | $24m | 3 | basketball |
| 4 | Alex Rodriguez | $35.2m | 3 | baseball |
| 5 | Mike Tyson | $48m | 1 | boxing |
| 6 | Allen Iverson | $14.3m | 2 | basketball |
| 7 | Marion Jones | $2.7m | 2 | track |
| 8 | Vince Carter | $4.2m | 1 | basketball |
| 9 | David Beckham | $10.6m | 1 | soccer |
| 10 | Ken Griffey, Jr. | $11.3m | 1 | baseball |

1. What is the purpose of this chart?


2. Which sport has the most amount of athletes represented on this chart? Why do you think this is so?


3. What do you think the panel votes means? Why are some people higher on the list even though they make less money?


4. What do you think about the salaries that athletes make? Do you think they deserve these salaries? Explain your answer.

# Do Athletes Make
# Too Much Money? *(cont.)*

## Document-Based Extension Activities

Work independently or in a small group to complete the following.

1. Attend a professional sporting event in your area.  (You may also watch one on television.)  Go to the event with questions in hand for you to observe and take notes.  Some questions to consider might include:

   - Is what the professional athletes are doing difficult to do?
   - Does their skill require training and hard effort?
   - Is their skill and technique providing a great service to our society?
   - How do the other people at the sporting event seem to feel about the athletes' skills?
   - How much money do you think the athletes should make in this event?
   - Do you think they deserve the money they make?
   - What is the cost involved in putting on the sporting event?
   - How much did the ticket cost to attend the sporting event?
   - How much do you think was spent in advertising for the sporting event?

2. Write a fictional newspaper article about the sporting event that you attended.  In the article, review the skill of the athletes involved.  Remember to answer the questions of who, what, where, when, why and how.  Research to find out how much money the athletes you saw make.

3. Interview an athlete or a coach.  Ask them what they think about the salaries that professional athletes make.  Has the price gone up as the years have gone by?  Get the opinion of the person you are interviewing as to why the price is so high.  How will this problem be addressed?

4. Analyze your findings.  Look at the results of your observations, your interviews, and your research.  How much money do you think athletes should make?  Do they make too much money?  Why or why not?  Write an essay on your opinion of how much money professional athletes make.  Select a title that will help you get your message across.  Be sure to list evidence in support of your opinion.

# Game Over!

It was the end of the era of air. Just one week after the NBA lockout was settled in 1999, hoops fans were saddened by the news that the game's greatest and most popular player, Michael Jordan, 35, was retiring from professional basketball.

"Mentally, I'm exhausted," Jordan explained at a news conference in Chicago. "I've accomplished everything I could as an individual."

Asked if he lost his desire to play, Jordan said that while "the desire is always going to be there . . . this is the perfect time for me to walk away from the game. I'm at peace with that."

Anyone who has ever seen Jordan play knows how he got his nickname, Air Jordan. Without wings and without wires, he seemed to fly toward the basket. Gravity? What's gravity?

Fans around the world were moved by his announcement. Jordan played 13 seasons in the NBA, all with the Chicago Bulls. He led them to six world championships. After being named the Rookie of the Year in 1984, he led the league in scoring ten times and was voted Most Valuable Player in the finals six times and in the regular season five times.

Jordan hangs up his sneakers with the highest scoring average in NBA history. His is third on the all-time scoring list, after Kareem Abdul-Jabbar and Wilt Chamberlain, who both had longer careers.

Of course, Jordan retired from the NBA once before, in 1993. Eighteen months later, after attempting to play minor league baseball, Jordan was back on the court with the Bulls.

Asked if he might return again, Jordan answered that while he was 99.9% certain that he wouldn't, he would "never say never." But this time, Jordan seems intent on staying retired. He can't wait to pick up his kids from school and "watch them play one on one." Said His Airness: "I'm just going to enjoy life and do some of the things I've never done before." If anyone has earned that right, it's Michael Jordan. We'll miss him. Unless he decides to come back—again.

# Game Over! *(cont.)*

**Directions:** Answer the questions. You may look at the article.

1. Who is His Airness? How did he get that name?



2. Describe in your own words how many people feel about Michael Jordan retiring.



3. Why is it significant that Jordan mentions he is 99.9% sure he is ready to retire?



4. What evidence can you list for why Michael Jordan feels it is time to retire?



5. Identify the motive for the author of this article leaving open the idea that Michael Jordan has retired before and maybe he will return again.



6. What reasons can you list for why Michael Jordan ought to stay playing basketball?



7. Do you agree with Michael Jordan's decision to retire? Why or why not?



8. Evaluate how you think the author did in presenting the facts and reasons for Jordan to retire.

# Game Over! *(cont.)*

Some might say that the Chicago Bulls have never been the same since Michael Jordan left. Below is the basketball team roster for the 2001–2002 season. Use the roster to answer the questions at the bottom of the page.

| NUM | PLAYER | POS | HT | WT | DOB | YRS |
|---|---|---|---|---|---|---|
| | *2001–02 Chicago Bulls Roster* | | | | | |
| 50 | Greg Anthony | G | 6-1 | 180 | 11/15/67 | 10 |
| 15 | Ron Artest | F | 6-7 | 246 | 11/13/79 | 2 |
| 44 | Dalibor Bagaric | C | 7-1 | 277 | 02/07/80 | 1 |
| 25 | Corey Benjamin (FA) | G | 6-6 | 205 | 02/24/78 | 3 |
| 3 | Tyson Chandler | C | 7-0 | 235 | 10/02/82 | R |
| 1 | Jamal Crawford | G | 6-5 | 175 | 03/20/80 | 1 |
| 2 | Eddy Curry | F-C | 6-11 | 285 | 12/05/82 | R |
| 21 | Marcus Fizer | F | 6-9 | 262 | 08/10/78 | 1 |
| 30 | Steve Goodrich (FA) | C | 6-10 | 220 | 03/18/76 | 1 |
| 11 | A.J. Guyton | G | 6-1 | 180 | 02/12/78 | 1 |
| 22 | Trenton Hassell | G | 6-5 | 200 | 03/04/79 | R |
| 20 | Fred Hoiberg (FA) | G | 6-5 | 210 | 10/15/72 | 6 |
| 25 | Sean Lampley | F | 6-7 | 225 | 09/09/79 | R |
| 5 | Ron Mercer | G-F | 6-7 | 210 | 05/18/76 | 4 |
| 40 | Brad Miller | C | 7-0 | 261 | 04/12/76 | 3 |
| 34 | Charles Oakley | F | 6-9 | 245 | 12/18/63 | 16 |
| 12 | Kevin Ollie | G | 6-2 | 195 | 12/27/72 | 4 |
| 32 | Eddie Robinson | F | 6-9 | 208 | 04/19/76 | 2 |
| 51 | Michael Ruffin | C-F | 6-8 | 248 | 01/21/77 | 2 |
| 12 | Dragan Tariac (FA) | CF | 6-11 | 270 | 05/09/73 | 1 |
| 43 | Jake Voskuhl | C | 6-11 | 245 | 11/01/77 | 1 |

(FA) – *free agent*
(R) – *rookie*

1. How many players are on this chart? If a basketball team has 5 players at a time, why are there so many on the team?

2. What do you think a free agent is? How many free agents are on this team roster?

3. Who is the tallest person on this team? How has Michael Jordan's height helped him in basketball?

4. How do you think the members of the Chicago Bulls felt about Michael retiring? What are the pros and cons of Michael retiring?

# Game Over! *(cont.)*

## Document-Based Extension Activities

Work independently or in a small group to complete the following.

1. How has Michael Jordan made a difference in the sport of basketball? How does whether or not Michael Jordan plays basketball affect the sport? Make a list of the achievements and contributions that Michael Jordan has made playing basketball. Are there other players who have played a significant role in basketball? Who are they and what contributions have they made?

2. Look back at the article, "Game Over!" How does Michael feel about retiring? Is he certain this is what he wants to do? What do you think would cause Michael to reevaluate his decision? We know that since this article Michael Jordan has come back to play basketball. Why do you think Michael Jordan returned?

3. Create a survey you can use to poll students in your school. Be sure to survey a large number of students to get an accurate view. Here are some questions to consider:

   - Do you think Michael Jordan should retire from basketball again?
   - How long do you think a professional athlete should be able to participate?
   - What are the pros and cons of staying in a sport for a long time?
   - How do you think sports affect the personal life of professional athletes?
   - What is the reason so many professional athletes retire so much earlier than non-athletes?
   - What do you think professional athletes should do once they retire? What contributions can they continue to make to our society?

4. Look back at your poll. Were you surprised by your findings, or did you get the answers you were expecting? What is the general consensus of the students in your school about professional athletes?

5. Write a newspaper article about the day Michael Jordan came back to basketball. What did his fans think? What was the name of the new team that he signed up with? Make a prediction on what Michael Jordan will do long after his playing days in basketball are over.

6. What should Michael Jordan do now? What advice do you have for Michael Jordan? Write a letter to Michael Jordan with your recommendations. What should he do and why? Try to incorporate the information you received from other students. What do you think Michael Jordan can do to continue to contribute to his sport?

# Answer Key

Many of the answers to the questions in this series are subjective, and your students may have different ones. Please note that these answers are suggestions and can be modified as needed.

## Page 17

1. Spectators saw 25,000 butterflies at one time.
2. A butterfly starts out as an egg, then it turns into a caterpillar, and then a butterfly. Depending on what time of year it is born, it can live up to nine months.
3. Loggers have cut down forests where monarchs spend their winter. Farmers use weed killers that destroy milkweed plants. Butterflies use these to eat. Weather conditions can affect the butterflies.
4. A dry spell means fewer plants to eat.
5. They are easily approachable, get along well with humans, and they don't need miles of room to live.
6. There won't be enough milkweed plants for butterflies to lay their eggs or eat. There will be fewer butterflies.
7. Answers will vary. He might track the weather reports, or work to keep loggers from destroying forests.
8. Answers will vary. The author did a good job of presenting how a butterfly lives, what it needs to survive, and the problems the butterfly is having in its migration pattern.

## Page 18

1. They begin in Canada and the northern states of the U.S. They migrate on down through the United States to Mexico. They might encounter weather patterns, other bugs, animals, etc.
2. People in these areas get to see these beautiful creatures. They might also have to deal with large numbers of butterflies in their fields, homes, etc.
3. Yes. Some people might be opposed to the butterflies coming in such large numbers. Most people would be in favor of the migration as it is a beautiful sight and the butterflies are harmless.

## Page 21

1. Cleopatra was queen of Egypt.
2. Floods and earthquakes buried Antirhodos more than 1,600 years ago.
3. Answers will vary. Cleopatra sought after power and got it. Power brings jealousy and deceit. Cleopatra died in love with Antony. She took her life.
4. Answers will vary.
5. She always seems to be involved in controversy and emotion.
6. Answers will vary.
7. Cleopatra could have chosen to try and fight the battle. She could have fought her brother.
8. Answers will vary. The author did a good job of sharing the information about Cleopatra and her history.

## Page 22

1. Hieroglyphics are a form of picture writing used in ancient Egypt.
2. Writing would take longer to write. The way writing would be taught would be different. Computer keyboards would have to be modified to accommodate the hieroglyphics as opposed to the letters. Reading and the way reading is taught would be different as well.
3. Answers will vary.
4. Answers will vary, as hieroglyphics can share many things about the culture. Answers might include foods, weather, protection, animals, and other parts of the Egyptian culture are shared through the hieroglyphics.

## Page 25

1. They were sent to the mediation center.
2. It usually takes students 15 minutes.
3. The mediation center is set up to allow students to come and discuss problems that are taking place with other students. Students are working with students to resolve discipline problems.
4. Answers will vary.
5. The mediation center gets students involved. The students seem to like the mediation center. The mediation center is more successful at handling discipline problems. Students are learning life skills that will help them in their lives.
6. Answers will vary.
7. Answers will vary. Perhaps you could run an anti-violence campaign at your school. Design posters that encourage students to get along and be considerate of each other.
8. Answers will vary.

## Page 26

1. This chart shows the cause and effects of arguments or disputes taking place in school.
2. Answers will vary.
3. DeAngela probably feels defensive. Ivory feels threatened and bothered. You can tell by how they react and how you would feel in that situation.
4. The cause is staples hit Ivory and he blames DeAngela. The effect is they are both sent to the mediation center.

## Page 29

1. To share the contributions and achievements that African Americans have made.
2. They covered themselves with Vaseline and then papier-mâché was applied to make the molds.
3. Answers will vary. You would probably feel inspired and amazed. You would also learn a lot.
4. Detroit was one of the last stops of the Underground Railroad. Many African Americans migrated to Detroit during the 1920s through the 1950s.
5. Answers will vary. This museum is specifically designed for African Americans.
6. In the article it states that African Americans are proud of it. The museum is educational and inspiring.
7. Answers will vary.
8. Answers will vary.

## Page 30

1. The carbon filament for the light bulb.
2. Answers will vary depending on the invention selected.
3. People might not be alive today without some of the inventions. Our lives have been enriched and made easier because of some of the inventions.
4. Answers will vary.

## Page 33

1. diamonds
2. An industrial diamond is a diamond that is flawed, oddly shaped, or too small for jewels.
3. Diamonds were formed billions of years ago. They were shot forth in boiling eruptions of melted rocks. These eruptions were smaller but more powerful than volcanoes.

# Answer Key *(cont.)*

4. A diamond costs a lot of money. It takes many years and lots of pressure to form a diamond.
5. It takes time and pressure. These forces turn black carbon into clear diamonds.
6. Answers will vary. Diamonds are perfectly shaped. Only a fraction of the 10 tons of natural diamonds mined each year are valuable diamonds.
7. Answers will vary.
8. Answers will vary.

## Page 34
1. These are the different products that are produced by the different continents.
2. Africa produces oil and diamonds. Europe produces textiles and oil. South America produces diamonds and emeralds. North America produces textiles. Asia produces tea and textiles. Australia produces only diamonds.
3. Answers will vary. They affect them a great deal. Their lifestyle and culture are often determined by the products they sell.

## Page 37
1. They are carrying backpacks that are too heavy.
2. His backpack was 20 pounds. He weighs 100 pounds.
3. The doctors think the backpacks are too heavy and are causing back and neck pain as a result.
4. Answers will vary.
5. Students are carrying more home from school. Homework assignments have changed through the years.
6. More and more kids are seeing the doctor about neck and back pain.
7. Answers will vary.
8. Answers will vary. Kids need to lighten their backpacks.

## Page 38
1. Blake. His maximum weight should be 12.5 lbs.
2. They are going to have neck and back pain.
3. Most kids complain if their backpacks are too heavy. Some don't care, and some may not even notice! You can tell by what kids say about their backpacks.
4. They can take their weight, and divide by 10.

## Page 41
1. Pavel was an 11-year-old Jewish boy, whose family was forced to leave its home. He died in the Holocaust.
2. April 23, 1998
3. The Holocaust was where Hitler and his government captured and killed millions of Jews throughout Europe.
4. A butterfly is free and can fly. But when it is caught, it is no longer free to fly. That is symbolic of what happened to the Jews and their freedom.
5. Pictures will vary.
6. The students felt connected to Pavel because of his poem about the butterfly. Seeing so many butterflies at one time brought a feeling of honor and excitement.
7. The students may not have connected in a personal way to the experience and story of Pavel.
8. Answers will vary. Allow students to share their response.

## Page 42
1. USSR
2. Answers will vary. Military should always be higher in war. Civilians should not die during war.
3. Because of the Holocaust. Millions and millions of people died as a result of the Holocaust.
4. Perhaps the war was carried out on the civilians. Perhaps the armies were weaker and therefore more civilians died.

## Page 45
1. She got the name from her work and effort to save the ocean. She also holds the world's record for the deepest dive by any human outside of a submarine.
2. These are underwater areas similar to national parks that are protected by the U.S. government.
3. She suggests that people stop polluting and over-using the ocean. She also suggests they stop using man-made fertilizers. She urges people to volunteer to clean a beach, and she also hopes people will get educated about the ocean.
4. They wash off fields into streams and eventually to the ocean. This encourages harmful overgrowth of algae and the spread of toxic germs that kill fish and cause health problems.
5. Answers will vary. There are many similarities, except that the ocean is underwater. People may be more aware of saving the rain forest.
6. Answers will vary.
7. Underwater species will become extinct. We may not even be aware of all the species because of how far down below the surface of the ocean they live.
8. Answers will vary.

## Page 46
1. The Pacific Ocean
2. It means a ditch.
3. She can know how far she needs to dive. She can use the information to research the deepest parts of the oceans.
4. It is hard to reach these species and see how they are doing. And if they need something, it is hard to get to them to assist.

## Page 49
1. A dam near three spectacular gorges or canyons, located in central China. It is still under construction.
2. He and his family need to move because they live where the Three Gorges Dam is being constructed.
3. The dam will threaten the habitats of hundreds of fish, plants, and animal species. People warn that blocking the river will create sewage backups and perhaps even more floods.
4. The Chinese government is building another dam and yet many of the dams built by the government have collapsed over the years. This one might collapse, as well.
5. Many people are forced to leave, habitats of animals, plants, and fish are threatened, and there is no guarantee that this dam will work. The citizens are not given a chance to speak out against their concerns.
6. Answers will vary.
7. Answers will vary.
8. Answers will vary.

## Page 50
1. approximately 400 miles
2. The area between Chongqing and Sandouping will be affected.

# Answer Key *(cont.)*

**Page 50** *(cont.)*
3. north/south
4. the Jialing River

**Page 53**
1. These are letters to the editor of a newspaper.
2. The American Library Association
3. One author thinks that laws should be passed providing libraries with funds to purchase software that blocks out offensive material on the Internet. The other author feels that this is imposing on the right of freedom. This author thinks that children should be taught how to avoid offensive material online.
4. Answers will vary. Look for answers that list support mentioned in the article.
5. Because it states that no one should be denied access to materials in the public libraries.
6. Answers will vary. Look for well thought out suggestions.
7. Essentially children would lose the opportunity to learn through the Internet. At the same time, they wouldn't be exposed to offensive material online.
8. Answers will vary.

**Page 54**
1. Symbols are a quick reference to locate items on the Internet.
2. Select icon *d*.
3. Pictures make it easier for children to use the Internet. Children don't have to know how to read if the symbols are used.
4. Answers will vary.

**Page 57**
1. The people of the Sandia Pueblo.
2. Spain
3. The group of citizens want to remain free to hang glide, hike, walk, and visit the Sandia Mountain any time they want without restrictions from the Native American tribe.
4. This gives the Native Americans the control over Sandia Mountain again.
5. He wants to be able to hike the mountain as he pleases with his family.
6. Answers will vary.
7. Answers will vary.
8. The author thinks that the people of the Sandia Pueblo should share the mountain. He thinks the 1998 ruling is wrong and should be reversed.

**Page 58**
1. This time line shows the events that have involved the Sandia Mountain and who has ownership of it.
2. They would be happy when the judge ordered 9,500 acres of the National Forest returned to the Sandia Pueblo. They would be sad when a group of citizens is working hard to reverse the judge's ruling.
3. They might be able to appeal the decision.
4. They can employ people to keep the mountain up and running. It would also make the Sandia Mountain available for all to enjoy.

**Page 61**
1. India
2. 1997

3. The Indian government is trying to save the tigers, and trying to keep the people out of the reserve. In the process, many children are dying and not getting the food and shelter they need.
4. Answers will vary.
5. Answers will vary.
6. Answers will vary. The government claims that the tigers and the people cannot live together on the Reserve.
7. Answers will vary. Look for answers that provide evidence and support for their opinion.
8. Answers will vary.

**Page 62**
1. The people look as though they are cooking food.
2. They live in families. They care for their young. They live where it is warm, based on their shelter and their clothing. They don't have very much money.
3. Yes, they do. They do not have secure homes. They live without running water or electricity. They look as though they don't use cars, computers, or other inventions of this century.
4. The danger might include that a villager might feel threatened by a tiger coming into the village and, thus, kill it.

**Page 65**
1. in Brazil
2. 1995
3. People are destroying the rain forest at a rapid pace. Scientists fear that animals and plant life will become extinct as a result of all the deforestation and destruction.
4. Prior to this, people weren't punished for destroying the rain forest. Maybe this ruling will help curb some of the destruction.
5. The heavy rainfall made it difficult for people to burn trees.
6. Perhaps they can make money with the items they take from the rain forest. Perhaps they use the products to make items to sell.
7. Answers will vary.
8. Answers will vary.

**Page 66**
1. square miles
2. 1995
3. The trend seems to be that the loss of rain forest is declining.
4. They can show how many thousands of square miles are being lost each year. They can show how their efforts have caused a decrease, and they can show the seriousness by the increases of the problem.

**Page 69**
1. It has increased by one degree in the past 100 years.
2. Scientists believe the earth is getting warmer.
3. Global warming is when pollution goes into the air. Part of the pollution is carbon dioxide gas. The carbon dioxide gets into the atmosphere and prevents the heat from the sun escaping from the earth. The heat keeps the earth warm.
4. Too much carbon dioxide keeps the sun's heat from leaving the atmosphere and so it keeps the air too warm.
5. the carbon dioxide, the atmosphere, and the heat of the sun
6. Answers will vary. Answers should have an explanation.
7. Answers will vary. Answers should have an explanation.
8. Stop pollution.

# Answer Key (cont.)

## Page 70

1. He has heard about it and he is wondering how it can be happening when it is so cold?
2. His father looks annoyed and probably frustrated by the comment.
3. Yes, they do. They wouldn't know to joke about it without having knowledge of it. The people seem to be wondering about the validity of global warming on such a cold day.
4. Yes. It would be difficult to catch the irony or the humor in these cartoons without knowing that global warming says the earth's temperature is increasing each year.

## Page 73

1. In 1992, 55% of children under two were vaccinated. In 1996, 75% of kids under two were immunized.
2. Childhood infectious diseases
3. Vaccines prevent children from getting serious illnesses that can cause injury or death.
4. The vaccines are making sure the immune system is able to run.
5. The number of childhood infectious diseases has gone down, which means less kids are getting sick with those illnesses.
6. Answers will vary.
7. Answers will vary.
8. Answers will vary.

## Page 74

1. Louisiana and Alaska
2. Michigan or Kansas because they have the lowest percentage rate of children being immunized in the United States.
3. They can educate the parents as to the benefits of having their children immunized. They can provide free immunizations.
4. The more educated a parent is, the more likely they are to get their children vaccinated.

## Page 77

1. He is a 13-year-old boy that traveled the world for a year fighting for kids' rights.
2. education
3. Children have to work in factories that are very hot. They work long hours, with strict bosses, and hardly any money for pay.
4. Craig is a kid himself.
5. There are children the world over that are personally experiencing it. There are samples and quotes in the article by children that are being used as child labor.
6. Answers will vary.
7. Answers will vary.
8. Answers will vary.

## Page 78

1. They are making clothing, working in mines, and are making shoes.
2. The countries that do not have a symbol next to them. For instance, the United States, Canada, Great Britain, etc.
3. Answers will vary. (China, Mexico, India, etc.)
4. Answers will vary, but based on the article, they don't like it. They hate it.

## Page 81

1. They were trying to get people to realize how important the buffalo were to them.
2. illegal hunting in Yellowstone National Park
3. They provided food, clothing and shelter.

4. If this herd dies, than there are no more free-roaming bison left.
5. They are afraid the bison will get their cattle sick.
6. Answers will vary. Students should support their answer.
7. Answers will vary.
8. Answers will vary.

## Page 82

1. The chart shows how much it would cost to purchase different types of bison.
2. A bull that is four years old is worth the most money.
3. Answers will vary.
4. Answers will vary.

## Page 85

1. Their parents don't realize the importance of an education. Some governments don't allow or encourage girls to attend school.
2. She has set up a boarding school for girls to live and get an education.
3. She learned how to read and write and make money growing kiwi fruit.
4. Answers will vary. Education opens doors and opens minds.
5. Traditionally it is expected that the boy will need education to provide for the family. Some countries believe that boys are a higher gender and deserve schooling while girls don't.
6. Answers will vary. Be sure responses show examples from the text to support the answers.
7. More girls would be sent to school. Children would be better cared for as mothers would have more knowledge and information.
8. Answers will vary.

## Page 86

1. The message is one of building confidence in other girls, a message of hope and a message that it is possible to achieve the impossible.
2. Mannejerka feels very strongly that girls need an education in life. They need it not only for themselves but for their families.
3. Mannejerka suggests that other countries step in to help her country educate girls.
4. Answers will vary.

## Page 89

1. to earn more money
2. He feels it is distracting kids from learning.
3. post signs, advertise, and sell their products
4. Answers will vary. The author is making the case that students are being brainwashed in school instead of being taught to make their own decisions.
5. If kids grow up hearing that Coke is the best drink, than they will buy Coke the rest of their lives.
6. Schools wouldn't receive the same large sums of money.
7. Answers will vary.
8. Answers will vary. Responses should include support for their opinions.

## Page 90

1. The message of the article is to let companies know they are no longer invited to be a part of the school district.
2. Answers will vary. Responses need examples to support opinion.

# Answer Key (cont.)

## Page 90 (cont.)

3. Soda and snacks are very popular items to kids and these companies stand to gain the most by being advertised and present in schools.
4. Answers will vary. The article may not ever have been written. The article might suggest positive things about brand name companies being mentioned in schools.

## Page 93

1. 26,000 people are hurt or killed each year; 8,000 children in Angola
2. An organization that is trying to rid the world of land mines. The group puts pressure on countries to eliminate land mines.
3. She has personally gone to persuade countries to ban land mines. She won the Nobel Peace Prize.
4. Answers will vary. Countries may not have a large enough army to protect itself. Some countries might need land mines where people cannot be.
5. It is much more dangerous to remove a land mine than it is to install one. There is more equipment and experienced people needed. That all costs money.
6. Some of these countries didn't sign the treaty because they still feel like these land mines are needed.
7. The U.S. says they need them along the North and South Korean border. Answers will vary on what they think the United States will do.
8. Answers will vary and should be supported with ideas.
9. Answers will vary.

## Page 94

1. Afghanistan
2. They have the most land mines still in place. These countries have been at war.
3. Answers will vary.
4. Answers will vary.

## Page 97

1. story problems that mention name brand products or companies
2. a lawyer in California; He didn't think it was a good idea.
3. The author feels that the students are being taken advantage of with the free advertising in the math textbooks.
4. The author feels that this can be distracting. The author feels that teachers are creative and can come up with their own ways to attract the attention of students.
5. The quote shows a specific example from a math textbook and allows the reader to see first-hand what is going on.
6. Answers will vary.
7. Answers will vary.
8. Answers will vary. Responses should include an explanation of the answer.

## Page 98

1. The school board policy is to prevent companies from selling things in their school district or their names being mentioned in curriculum or lessons.
2. Answers will vary. Be sure the answer is supported with examples.
3. Answers will vary. Schools are feeling pressure from parents and other groups about the free advertising. Students' pros and cons will vary.
4. Answers will vary. Companies can show examples of how their money spent on schools has benefited and improved the education of the students.

## Page 101

1. The topic is whether or not athletes make too much money.
2. The article states athletes work only a few hours a week, while others work at least 40 hours a week.
3. Answers will vary.
4. Answers will vary.
5. Answers will vary.
6. Professional teams would have to find another way to pay athletes. Student responses should include how the loss of that money would affect salaries.
7. Answers will vary.
8. Answers will vary.

## Page 102

1. The purpose of the chart is to show the top ten most valuable sports figures.
2. Basketball has the most athletes on the list, perhaps because the sport is such a big moneymaker for the teams.
3. Answers will vary. The panel vote might mean the number of people on the panel that voted for this athlete. They are placed on the list based on their number of votes.
4. Answers will vary. Students need to explain their answer.

## Page 105

1. Michael Jordan. He got the name because he can jump so high.
2. Many people are sad and disappointed. Jordan will be missed.
3. It leaves room for him to come out of retirement again. It indicates that he is not completely sure.
4. Answers may include that he is mentally tired, he has accomplished his goals, etc.
5. The author is really hoping that Michael Jordan will come back to basketball.
6. Answers will vary. Answers may include that Michael Jordan is so talented and has so much more left to offer basketball. Other great players played longer than Jordan.
7. Answers will vary.
8. Answers will vary. Answers should include examples from the text.

## Page 106

1. There are 21 players listed on this chart. There are so many more than five because you have to account for injuries or other reasons why players can't play. Also, there are a certain number of players for each position who are trained and coached for that specific position. Players also need rest periods.
2. Answers will vary. A free agent is a player who does not have a contract with the current team and can choose to go to another team if an offer is made. There are four free agents on this team.
3. The tallest person is Dalibor Bagaric. He is seven feet and one inch tall. His height has helped him to jump higher and obtain his Air Jordan name.
4. Answers will vary. Responses should include reasons for both pros and cons. Some other players might get to play or shine now that Michael is gone. Michael leaving takes away a bit from the Chicago Bulls team.